HUMAN EVENTS

A R Gurney

BROADWAY PLAY PUBLISHING INC
New York
www.broadwayplaypublishing.com
info@broadwayplaypublishing.com

HUMAN EVENTS
© Copyright 2001 by A R Gurney

All rights reserved. This work is fully protected under the copyright laws of the United States of America. No part of this publication may be photocopied, reproduced, stored in a retrieval system, or transmitted, in any form or by any means, electronic, mechanical, recording, or otherwise, without the prior permission of the publisher. Additional copies of this play are available from the publisher.

Written permission is required for live performance of any sort. This includes readings, cuttings, scenes, and excerpts. For amateur and stock performances, please contact Broadway Play Publishing Inc. For all other rights please contact Jonathan Lomma, W M F, 212 903-1550.

Cover photo: T Charles Erickson

I S B N: 978-0-88145-201-3
First printing: September 2001
This printing: May 2017

Book design: Marie Donovan
Page make-up: Adobe InDesign
Original copy editing: Sue Gilad
Typeface: Palatino
Printed and bound in the U S A

This play is based on the author's novel *Entertaining Strangers*, published by Doubleday, 1977.

HUMAN EVENTS was first produced at the George Street Playhouse (David Saint, Artistic Director; Michael Stotts, Managing Director) in New Brunswick NJ, opening on 6 January 2001, with the following cast and creative contributors:

PORTER PLATT..Jack Gilpin
CHRISTOPHER SIMPSON...........................Patrick Fitzgerald
NANCY PLATT.......................................Kathleen McNenny
SEYMOUR BLUM ....Tim Jerome
ANITA DE VITA.. Anne De Salvo
STUDENTS............. Florence Clutch & Daniel Domingues

Director...David Saint
Set design..James Youmans
Costume design.. David Murin
Lighting design..Kenneth Posner
Sound design..Chris Bailey
Production stage manager ....Patti McCabe

CHARACTERS & SETTING

PORTER PLATT
CHRISTOPHER SIMPSON
NANCY PLATT
SEYMOUR BLUM
ANITA DE VITA
Two or more STUDENTS, *male and female, of various ethnicity, to play assorted roles, as well as to assist with set changes*

This play takes place in and around a large technological institute located along the Charles River in Cambridge, Massachusetts. The overall surround should suggest rather cold and forbidding contemporary architecture. The central location is a professor's office, containing a desk, a couple of chairs, and bookcases behind. This area should appear to be a kind of island of warmth within its cold surroundings. Somewhere there might be displayed a family photograph, but otherwise the desk and bookcases are loaded with journals, manuscripts, and books. Many of these are paperbacks, stuffed with notes and clippings. On a wall of this office, if there is a wall, there might be a poster of an exhibition of American painting at the Boston Museum of Fine Arts. Other playing spaces should be defined primarily by light, but whatever the design, the overall set should allow for minimum stage machinery and maximum fluidity.

PRODUCTION NOTES

COSTUMES:

Since the play is set in the early 1970s, there should be some attempt to suggest the period through hairstyles and costumes. On the other hand, the institute is a conservative place. The faculty wears for the most part what faculties usually wear, and even the students are not particularly trendy. To focus on the distinctive costume styles of the period would make the play seem more quaint than relevant. As far as props are concerned, the faculty carries casual and battered bookbags while the students might wear plastic pencil shields and carry slide rules and large science tomes rather than the usual paperbacks.

MUSIC:

There are a number of music cues. Whatever songs are used should evoke the period, cover the shift from one scene to another, and if possible comment on the action.

For David Saint, with affection and appreciation.

"When in the course of human events it becomes necessary for one people to dissolve the political bands which have connected them with another, …a decent respect for the opinions of mankind requires that they should declare the causes…"
The Declaration of Independence

ACT ONE

(Before rise: music, something that immediately recalls the early seventies)

(At rise: PORTER PLATT *comes on, as if arriving at work. He wears the conventional uniform of the teaching trade: corduroy trousers, rumpled tweed jacket, tattersall shirt, possibly a tie, and rubber-soled, comfortable leather shoes. His hair and his sideburns are just long enough to suggest a minor concession to the fashions of the days. He carries a bookbag.)*

PORTER: *(To audience)* I used to think I was a gentle man. Violence was something others did unto others, somewhere apart from me. Oh, I could get mad occasionally, and yell at my wife, or swear at my kids, but violent? That I didn't think I was. *(He arrives at his office.)* And I used to think I had the perfect job. I was a Professor—all right, an Associate Professor, but with tenure—O K, when tenure was easier to get—in the Department of Humanities at a major technological institution in Cambridge, Massachusetts. *(He opens his bookbag, takes out his books and notes, settles into his chair to prepare a class.)* There I was, secure for life, surrounded by good books and bright students and learned colleagues and fringe benefits, commuting casually along the gentle Charles River from the green and pleasant suburb where I lived. And then, for reasons to be presented here, I suddenly found myself seething with anger, committing rape, and attempting murder, all within a single second semester. *(Displays a thick, dog-eared paperback copy of* The Odyssey, *stuffed with notes and bookmarks)* My downfall began on a Friday, early in the fall term, early in the 1970s, as I was preparing for my twelve o'clock class on *The Odyssey*, which I had taught for several years. *(Settles at his desk)* I was trying to crank up something new to say about Book Six, where the hero, lost, naked and alone, finds himself washed up onto the shores of a strange new land...

(CHRISTOPHER SIMPSON *sticks his head in the "door". He wears a dark gray suit, cut in the tight-waisted English fashion, along with a white shirt and dull tie. He carries a blue-and-white overnight flight bag marked with the letters BOAC.)*

CHRIS: *(English accent)* I beg your pardon.

PORTER: *(Startled)* Jesus.

CHRIS: Sorry. Did I startle you?

PORTER: I was lost in my book.

CHRIS: I fear I'm lost as well. I'm looking for the Department of Humanities.

PORTER: That's where you are.

CHRIS: Here? These bleak and empty halls?

PORTER: Well, you see, most people are over at the Boston Common protesting the Viet Nam war.

CHRIS: But not you.

PORTER: I hate to cut a class.

CHRIS: I suppose Professor Seymour Blum is protesting, too.

PORTER: Seymour? No. I believe he's gone to New York for the Jewish holidays. He should be back Monday.

CHRIS: I had an appointment for eleven o'clock.

ACT ONE

PORTER: With Seymour? Here? Today? It must have slipped his mind.

CHRIS: I fly back Sunday night.

PORTER: Back?

CHRIS: To England.

PORTER: England! Good Lord. You flew across the Atlantic for an appointment with Seymour, and he doesn't show? Come in and sit down!

CHRIS: Ah, but you're preparing a class.

PORTER: Never mind. Come in, come in.

CHRIS: Thank you. *(He comes in.)*

PORTER: I'm Porter Platt.

CHRIS: Christopher Simpson here.

(They shake hands.)

PORTER: Coffee or something, Chris?

CHRIS: Tea would be lovely.

PORTER: Tea. I should have guessed. Tea. *(He finds a grubby old teabag in a desk drawer, turns on an electric kettle.)*

CHRIS: I suspect you're what the Americans call a hawk, rather than a dove.

PORTER: Because I'm not protesting? Oh hell. I'm as much against the war as anyone else. I just get a little tired of all that yelling.

CHRIS: Ah yes…Better by far to nestle into a book. What are you teaching?

PORTER: *(Showing him the book)* The Odyssey.

CHRIS: Magnificent Homer.

PORTER: It's for a staff-taught course. Required of all freshmen. First semester: "The Classical Tradition."

Second semester: "The Judeo-Christian Alternative." We call it "The Old One-Two."

CHRIS: I've heard you Americans do that sort of thing.

PORTER: It began at the University of Chicago. Took root at Columbia, and many other places. Gives us a kind of cultural base. Which you already have in England.

CHRIS: I suppose we do...

PORTER: But hey, I'll bet there's some mistake about your appointment. Seymour wouldn't just shove off. Do you have a letter or something?

CHRIS: I have several. *(He hands* PORTER *a sheaf of letters from his breast pocket. Some are typewritten, some are neatly handwritten.)* Xeroxed copies of my own correspondence, and Professor Seymour Blum's replies. In chronological order.

PORTER: *(Looking at the top document, which is handwritten)* I must say you write well, Chris. I mean, your penmanship.

CHRIS: One small way of asserting oneself against the tyranny of the typewriter.

PORTER: *(Gesturing with his fist)* Right on! *(Reads)* Queen's College, Oxford...I'm already impressed.

CHRIS: Ah well.

PORTER: *(Reads; looks up)* Here you ask about a job.

CHRIS: Yes.

PORTER: I don't think we have any openings, Chris.

CHRIS: Read on, please.

PORTER: *(Reads)* Eton! ...You went to Eton?

CHRIS: After a fashion.

PORTER: You can't do better than Eton and Oxford.

ACT ONE

CHRIS: Perhaps I can.

PORTER: By coming here?

CHRIS: This is the belly of the beast, isn't it? The heart of American science and technology.

PORTER: For me, it boils down to trying to reach a bunch of bright, hard-working kids with little time for the liberal arts.

CHRIS: That's the challenge, isn't it?

PORTER: That is the challenge. *(Reads a typed reply)* But Seymour writes that nothing's available…

CHRIS: Yes.

PORTER: *(Reads another handwritten note)* So you inquire if the picture might change.

CHRIS: Yes.

PORTER: And Seymour says… *(Reads another typed letter)* "Highly unlikely"…"shrinking budget"…"large number of qualified Americans…" *(To CHRIS)* All of which is true, Chris.

CHRIS: Read what I write next.

PORTER: *(Reads another handwritten note)* "I hope to drop by your office on Friday, September seventeenth at eleven A M unless I hear to the contrary." *(Looks up)* That's all?

CHRIS: Isn't it enough?

PORTER: Hey Chris. This is hardly an appointment.

CHRIS: One might call it a tacit appointment.

PORTER: In England maybe…

CHRIS: I heard nothing to the contrary.

PORTER: I know, but to fly all the way over…

CHRIS: I obviously assumed too much.

(The kettle whistles.)

PORTER: I guess the water's ready for the tea. *(He makes tea.)* Where are you staying, Chris?

CHRIS: It seems I'm not.

PORTER: I mean, while you're here.

CHRIS: Oh I'll find some place. *(Sips his tea fussily)* Lovely. Spot on. *(He gingerly removes the grubby teabag.)*

PORTER: What will you do until Sunday night?

CHRIS: Do? Here? In the Athens of America? I plan to visit your magnificent Gardner Museum. I hope to hear the Mozart Twenty-First Piano Concerto at Symphony Hall. I'd like to see Salem or Concord on Sunday.

PORTER: I live in Concord.

CHRIS: Where they fired the shot heard 'round the world?

PORTER: Want to stay with us?

CHRIS: Us being?

PORTER: Me. My wife. My kids.

CHRIS: Oh well.

PORTER: Of course you will. *(Grabbing the telephone; push-button dials)* Chris, I'm doing three things. First, I'm calling my wife...

(Sound of a telephone ringing. NANCY, PORTER's *wife, comes on, sewing a button on some garment. She doesn't hold an actual telephone. During this,* CHRIS *might peruse the books in* PORTER's *bookcase.)*

NANCY: Hello?

CHRIS: Hi, sweetheart.

NANCY: I can't talk long. *(Glancing off)* The man's here fixing the hot water heater.

PORTER: I'm bringing someone home for dinner.

ACT ONE

NANCY: We're having spaghetti.

PORTER: He's from England, sweetheart.

NANCY: Which means what?

PORTER: I don't know. Something English.

NANCY: We've got English muffins.

PORTER: O K. Good. Have them for breakfast. Because I've asked him to spend the night. Two nights actually. He's sort of stranded.

CHRIS: *(At bookcase)* Oh now.

NANCY: Where will we put him?

PORTER: How about the boys' room?

NANCY: They're having a gang in for a sleep-over after the soccer game.

PORTER: Postpone it. Put them in with Betsy.

NANCY: She'll scream. She thinks she's having her period.

PORTER: Say guests come first.

CHRIS: Oh dear.

NANCY: The house is a pit, Porter! Mrs Knoblock hasn't been here since the dog had diarrhea.

PORTER: Get the kids to pitch in.

NANCY: They'll make it worse.

PORTER: Just change the sheets, then. And sweetheart, could you possibly iron them, do you think?

NANCY: *Iron* the *sheets*?

PORTER: He's English, Nancy!

CHRIS: *(From the bookcase)* Oh now, now.

PORTER: I'd help, but we have a staff meeting at four.

NANCY: I can't play hostess all weekend, Porter. *(Calls off)* Get that cat off the counter! *(To* PORTER*)* I have to write my report.

PORTER: *(To* CHRIS*; hand over receiver)* She's working on her master's degree on health and nutrition.

CHRIS: Fascinating.

NANCY: *(On phone)* Shit, Porter. I wish you didn't spring things on me.

PORTER: *(Back on phone)* You said something, darling?

NANCY: I said shit.

PORTER: *(Wincing)* Watch the language, sweetie. He's from Eton and Oxford.

NANCY: Yes, and I'm from the State University at Buffalo! *(She goes off.)*

CHRIS: I can easily find other lodgings.

PORTER: Nonsense. I'll give you the Grand tour. Concord and Salem and Beacon Hill.

CHRIS: Lovely.

PORTER: And here's the second thing I'm going to do. *(Showing him his book)* I'm going to take you to my class on *The Odyssey*.

CHRIS: I'd be delighted.

PORTER: Some of them might be out protesting the war. We might be talking to a small remnant.

CHRIS: As Christ said, whenever two or three are gathered together...

PORTER: *(Gathering up his books)* Maybe you'd be willing to say a few words.

CHRIS: My pleasure.

PORTER: *(As they walk)* You'll like the students, actually. We've worked out a gentleman's agreement. I try to

ACT ONE

make the subject entertaining. They try to stay awake. I try to keep the assignments manageable. They try to do half of them.

CHRIS: Sounds very agreeable.

PORTER: Though I have to say, Chris, I've been losing my spark lately. *(He stops.)* Maybe I've taught the course too long, but I'm starting to feel like an echo chamber. For instance, in Book Six, where we are now—

CHRIS: What's the third thing?

PORTER: Third thing?

CHRIS: You said you'd do three things. Home, class… What's the third?

PORTER: I was thinking of arranging an informal interview, so you could meet some of my other colleagues.

CHRIS: I'd like that.

PORTER: But you'll be gone on Monday.

CHRIS: We could do it tomorrow.

PORTER: Saturday? I doubt if anyone will come in.

CHRIS: You might point out that I have traveled over three thousand miles.

PORTER: True.

CHRIS: So if a position should emerge, at least they'll know who I am.

PORTER: I'll get on the horn this evening.

CHRIS: Thank you. Now where do we meet this class?

PORTER: *(Indicating)* Right down this hall…

(CHRIS *continues on offstage as* PORTER *peels off.*)

PORTER: *(To audience)* And it was a great class! Not because of me, I hasten to add. After introducing

Mister Christopher Simpson, of Eton and Oxford, I suddenly felt awkward and self-conscious. But then Chris stood up. Within five minutes he had the students seeing them*selves* as Odysseus, washed up on this strange island called college, forced to survive on their own intelligence. Then he led them to see that *he* was an Odysseus, too, another stranger in a strange land. Snd that carried them into a discussion of human hospitality, and why the gods viewed it as an essential virtue...

(Enthusiastic voices of STUDENTS *from off)*

PORTER: And after class, they gathered around him and talked some more...

(CHRIS *comes back on.*)

PORTER: Bravo, Chris! You done good.

CHRIS: I'd have done better, had I time to prepare.

PORTER: O K. Let's drive out to the cradle of the Revolution where you'll meet my family, warts and all...

(They go out, as music comes up.)

(Lights define another corridor. A STUDENT *comes on. He sits, as if against a wall, thumbing through a course catalogue. After a moment,* PROFESSOR SEYMOUR BLUM *comes on. He is more formally dressed than* PORTER.*)*

SEYMOUR: *(To* STUDENT*)* Waiting to see me?

STUDENT: I think so. If you are... *(He checks his catalogue.)* Professor Seymour Blum.

SEYMOUR: I am indeed. You can remember my name because I see more blum than anyone else around.

STUDENT: *(Gathering his books; getting up)* It says here you're in charge of The Old One-Two.

ACT ONE

SEYMOUR: I am primus inter pares. First among equals. We all teach it, we all run it.

STUDENT: I want to shift to a different section next term.

SEYMOUR: You're unhappy with your instructor?

STUDENT: I think I can do better.

SEYMOUR: You can petition through Mrs Ryan, in Department Headquarters.

STUDENT: Thank you, sir.

(SEYMOUR *starts out, then stops.*)

SEYMOUR: May I ask what section you're in now?

STUDENT: Professor Porter Platt's.

SEYMOUR: You don't like Professor Platt?

STUDENT: I like Professor Simpson better.

SEYMOUR: Professor who?

STUDENT: The English guy who did a guest spot last Friday.

SEYMOUR: He's not on the faculty.

STUDENT: He might be, next term.

SEYMOUR: Who told you that?

STUDENT: He did. After class.

SEYMOUR: I'm afraid he misled you. (*Starts out again, then stops again*) Tell me. What was so good about him?

STUDENT: He makes you think.

SEYMOUR: About what?

STUDENT: Yourself.

SEYMOUR: Doesn't Professor Platt?

STUDENT: He makes you think about the book.

SEYMOUR: You find yourself more interesting than Homer?

STUDENT: Who doesn't?

SEYMOUR: I don't. I find you somewhat less interesting.

STUDENT: I meant...

SEYMOUR: I know what you meant... Look. What I find more interesting than either one of us is how Homer connects with other books across the centuries. Great books always talk to each other, and when we listen in, we acquire a better way of thinking—about ourselves and the world.

STUDENT: Good point.

SEYMOUR: Thank you.

STUDENT: Maybe I'll switch to your section.

SEYMOUR: I wouldn't. I made it sound too easy.

STUDENT: What's your grading policy?

SEYMOUR: My grading policy?

STUDENT: What percent of As do you give? Or do you mark on a bell-shaped curve?

SEYMOUR: I simply reward the good and punish the bad.

STUDENT: I'll stay with Platt. I need a B to keep my deferment with the draft board.

SEYMOUR: As a New York waiter would say, "Good choice."

(The STUDENT goes, as SEYMOUR goes toward PORTER's office. PORTER enters hurriedly from another direction.)

SEYMOUR: *(Checking his watch)* I thought you had office hours this morning.

PORTER: I was at Logan airport till one A M.

SEYMOUR: Seeing your friend off?

ACT ONE

PORTER: Right.

(PORTER *Goes into his office;* SEYMOUR *follows.)*

SEYMOUR: I find myself seething with righteous indignation.

PORTER: About what?

SEYMOUR: About the fact that you called a meeting of the Appointments Committee on Saturday morning.

PORTER: It was an informal meeting.

SEYMOUR: It was an illegal meeting. Since I wasn't there. Nor were several others.

PORTER: I thought folks should meet him. Before he went back.

SEYMOUR: There are no jobs available, Porter! None! Which is what I wrote the gentleman. Twice.

PORTER: A slot might open up.

SEYMOUR: If one does, I have a folder full of applicants who are infinitely more qualified.

PORTER: More qualified than Eton and Oxford?

SEYMOUR: What has he written?

PORTER: I don't know.

SEYMOUR: By their works shall ye know them.

PORTER: Everyone who met him was extremely impressed.

SEYMOUR: Fine. Then let's review the bidding, shall we? In the unlikely case that an opening occurs, I'll invite him to apply. I'll also ask him to submit his written work. I will go on to solicit the opinions of reputable colleagues in his field. Then, if all goes well, I'll schedule a regular interview with all of us in the course. After which, we will compare and contrast him and his work to other applicants.

PORTER: O K, O K, O K.

SEYMOUR: Speaking of written work, how's yours coming?

PORTER: Fine.

SEYMOUR: The Dean asked me to remind you that you got your tenure on the assumption that you'd continue to publish.

PORTER: I'm working on a book, Seymour.

SEYMOUR: Yeah, yeah. Your novel.

PORTER: No, seriously. Something academic. I've even got a title. *The Neglected Sector*...colon...*The Family in American Fiction*.

SEYMOUR: I don't like your colon.

PORTER: I think that most American writers have neglected family life. Our heavy hitters either condemn it or ignore it. I'm asking why.

SEYMOUR: And you're making progress?

PORTER: I am. And I know I'm on the right track, after meeting Chris Simpson. He made me think of all those cozy families in Jane Austen and Dickens, versus the lack of same in Melville, or Twain, or Faulkner. What do you think?

SEYMOUR: I think you should write it down. And get it published. And earn your promotion to full professor. What I don't think is that you should spend these crucial years with all bright promise unfulfilled.

PORTER: What's that from? "All bright promise unfulfilled."

SEYMOUR: Me. It's from me. I just made it up. Do you like it?

(ANITA *DE VITA comes on. She wears vaguely bohemian clothes.*)

ACT ONE

ANITA: Sorry to interrupt, but I have some very sad news!

SEYMOUR: Pray put us in possession of it.

ANITA: Arnie Bernstein has been drafted.

PORTER: No.

ANITA: His graduate school deferment ran out, so they made him 1-A.

PORTER: But he's teaching a section of The Old One-Two.

ANITA: His draft board decided it was not essential.

SEYMOUR: How little they know!

ANITA: He's planning to escape to Canada right after he's taught the anti-war passages in *The Oresteia*.

SEYMOUR: A teacher to the last.

PORTER: I'll miss the guy.

ANITA: So will I. He was more fun.

SEYMOUR: More fun than what?

ANITA: More fun than my ex-husband, actually.

SEYMOUR: That's not saying much.

ANITA: Neither did my ex-husband.

SEYMOUR: We sound like a sit-com. Quickly, stop us, Porter.

PORTER: Who'll teach Arnie's section of the course?

SEYMOUR: We'll have to hire another graduate student.

PORTER: How about Christopher Simpson?

ANITA: Who?

PORTER: The English guy you interviewed on Saturday.

ANITA: Oh right. Yes. Why not him?

SEYMOUR: That was not a valid interview.

PORTER: You liked him, didn't you, Anita?

ANITA: He seemed good enough.

SEYMOUR: "Good enough" is not good enough, Anita. Remember, we get our students for so little time. They deserve the best.

ANITA: Well excuse *me*, Seymour. I'm just a lowly lecturer, without tenure, trying to support two young children on a single salary and no benefits.

SEYMOUR: You're an excellent teacher, Anita.

ANITA: Much good it does me at promotion time.

PORTER: Let me call Chris, Seymour.

SEYMOUR: No. I'll notify the placement offices at Harvard, B U, and Brandeis. We'll schedule interviews.

PORTER: For one small section? Of a staff-taught course? With the term already underway? Help me out here, Anita.

ANITA: That does seem kind of silly, Seymour.

PORTER: We're talking Eton and Oxford here.

ANITA: And Porter's seen him teach.

PORTER: And he's terrific!

ANITA: As if good teaching made any difference around here.

PORTER: Let me at least find out if he's available.

SEYMOUR: Sorry. I intend to round up the usual suspects. *(Starts out)*

PORTER: Why don't you like the guy, Seymour?

SEYMOUR: Because I know the type. He's another one of those English amateurs who wander through the world, sneaking into Mecca, climbing Mount Everest, and leaving trails of debris behind them.

ANITA: You make him sound even more exciting.

ACT ONE

SEYMOUR: The man doesn't understand the word No!

PORTER: Neither did Odysseus.

SEYMOUR: Neither did Gregory of Capadocia. *(He goes.)*

ANITA: Who was Gregory of Capadocia?

PORTER: No one. He makes things up.

(Pause)

ANITA: Porter…

PORTER: Yes?

ANITA: This Christopher Simpson… Is he married, do you know? I didn't notice a ring.

PORTER: I didn't look.

ANITA: I did.

PORTER: He never mentioned a wife.

ANITA: Porter, I'm going to tell you something.

PORTER: Go ahead.

ANITA: Arnie Bernstein and I were lovers.

PORTER: I knew that.

ANITA: Who told you?

PORTER: You did. At The Old One-Two Spring party.

ANITA: Oh those parties! …Anyway, he's seventeen years younger than I am. But so was Frederic Chopin with George Sand.

PORTER: These are passionate times.

ANITA: Actually, we got involved because of The Old One-Two. Neither one of us was at home with the material. My thing is Keats, and Arnie wrote his thesis on Dostoyevski. And there we were thrashing around in Thucydides. So we started meeting to figure out how to teach it.

PORTER: The course sure brings us together.

ANITA: It sure does. By the time we reached the second semester, Arnie and I were Paolo and Francesca, in Dante's *Inferno*, falling in love over a book.

PORTER: Life imitates art.

ANITA: I'm going to tell you something else, Porter.

PORTER: Go ahead.

ANITA: My teaching is terrible if I don't have sex.

PORTER: You told me that, too.

ANITA: At the party? Did I go on to tell you that after my husband left, I lost half my students in a course on Keats?

PORTER: No you didn't.

ANITA: On the other hand, you might recall that recently I was nominated for the undergraduate teaching prize.

PORTER: Because of Arnie.

ANITA: Because of Arnie.

PORTER: My compliments to you both.

ANITA: I'm a teacher, Porter. I survive on teaching. It's what I do. I'll never publish much, and I'm a hopeless administrator. With Arnie gone, I'm scared I'll run out of steam. Which is why I asked you about...what's his name again?

PORTER: Christopher Simpson.

ANITA: He was a nice-looking man.

PORTER: Yes.

ANITA: But they say the English are terrible in bed.

PORTER: I wouldn't know.

ANITA: If Seymour has his way, we could end up with some overqualified dyke from Brandeis.

ACT ONE

PORTER: It's happened before.

ANITA: And your man seemed ready—I mean, to teach.

PORTER: He is.

ANITA: Maybe, since people have met him, we could call a meeting, and take a vote, and persuade Seymour to invite...I keep forgetting his name...

PORTER: Chris.

ANITA: ...invite Chris to assume Arnie's position—I mean, on the staff.

PORTER: I'm ready to call England.

ANITA: *(Starting out)* I'm feeling better already.

PORTER: Don't get your hopes up, Anita. He's probably already committed.

ANITA: Don't say that! Don't! Not when I have to teach in twenty minutes! *(She goes.)*

PORTER: *(To audience)* So we met that afternoon, and made the arguments, and Seymour bowed to the majority opinion...

SEYMOUR: *(Coming into PORTER's office)* Like Socrates in *The Apology*, I have enjoyed the fruits of a democratic society. Therefore I must submit to the will of the people, even if it leads to my own death...

PORTER: This won't kill you, Seymour.

SEYMOUR: There are many ways to die.

PORTER: *(Flipping through his Rolodex)* Fortunately he left his number. *(He begins to dial.)*

SEYMOUR: Make it brutally clear: one section...of one course...for one term... Minimum salary... No benefits...no travel pay...

(The sound of an English telephone ringing)

SEYMOUR: ...and he shares an office with Natalie Katz...

PORTER: I doubt frankly that he'll come.

SEYMOUR: I pray fervently that he doesn't. *(He goes off.)*

(More ringing. A woman's VOICE *answers; English lower-class accent.)*

VOICE: *(Over speakers)* State your business, luv.

PORTER: May I speak to Mr Simpson, please?

VOICE: Hold on, ducky.

PORTER: *(To audience)* One of those endearing English landladies. I saw her scurrying to fetch Chris, who was probably sipping port at the end of a burnished oaken table, discussing A E Housman with V S Pritchett and C P Snow...

CHRIS: *(Over speakers)* Yes?

PORTER: The Voice of America, Chris.

CHRIS: Identify yourself, please.

PORTER: Porter Platt. Remember?

CHRIS: Ah hah.

PORTER: Who was that lady? Your coy mistress?

CHRIS: This is a poor connection.

PORTER: *(To audience)* I told him about the job, with all its limitations.

CHRIS: Would you repeat the specifics?

PORTER: I admit it's a little insulting, Chris. And I'm sure you're already committed for the—

CHRIS: I'll take it.

PORTER: What?

CHRIS: I said I'll take it.

ACT ONE 21

PORTER: *(Hanging up phone; to audience)* And he did. And he took me.

(Music. NANCY *comes on, carrying a liquor bottle with a silver bow around it.)*

NANCY: Look what he brought you. A bottle of port.

PORTER: From the private cellars of Queen's College?

NANCY: *(Looking at a tag)* From the duty-free shop at Gatwick Airport.

PORTER: Oh.

NANCY: He brought an opera for me. *Don Giovanni.* London Records.

PORTER: You don't like opera.

NANCY: He says I will.

PORTER: Where is he now?

NANCY: Taking a shower. Or rather a bahth. Do you think he expects to stay a while?

PORTER: We've got room.

NANCY: The carpenters start next week, Porter.

PORTER: *(To audience)* We were having open-heart surgery on our kitchen—to make it a more of a family room.

NANCY: We'll be cooking off a hot plate in the cellar. He'll be miserable!

PORTER: He's used to that.

*(*CHRIS *comes on, in more informal clothes.)*

PORTER: Aren't you, Chris?

CHRIS: Used to…?

PORTER: Living in cellars. Braving the London Blitz.

CHRIS: I wasn't there.

PORTER: Oh? Were you a country boy? Where from? Stow-on-the-Wold? Mill on the Floss? Toad in the Hole?

CHRIS: Salisbury, actually.

PORTER: Salisbury? With its magnificent twelfth-century cathedral?

CHRIS: Salisbury, the capitol of Rhodesia.

NANCY: Rhodesia?

PORTER: Rhodesia, Africa?

CHRIS: It's a lovely place actually. Despite its deplorable racial situation.

PORTER: Rhodesia, eh?

CHRIS: I'm sure I told you.

PORTER: Maybe I didn't hear you.

NANCY: Maybe all you heard was Eton and Oxford.

CHRIS: Well said, Nancy.

NANCY: What say we eat before the wrecking ball arrives.

CHRIS: Hear, hear...

(CHRIS *follows* NANCY *off.* PORTER *remains.*)

PORTER: *(To audience)* Rhodesia... Soon to become Zimbabwe... But at that time: Rhodesia. *(Pause)* Well hell. What's wrong with Rhodesia, I thought. Lovely name, lovely place... The awesome splendor of Victoria Falls...vast parks teeming with wild game, pursued by Rhodesian ridge-backs...

(SEYMOUR *comes on.*)

SEYMOUR: *(Reading a document)* Did you know your man was Rhodesian? His resumé finally arrived.

(*They move toward* PORTER's *office.*)

ACT ONE

PORTER: I see that as a plus. It means he's not some upper-class twit out of Evelyn Waugh. Solid colonial stock, empire-building grit. Cry the Beloved Rhodesia.

SEYMOUR: *(Reading from document)* Won a Rhodes scholarship to do graduate work at Oxford... Supported himself by coaching drama and rugby at... tad-da Eton.

PORTER: Good for him.

SEYMOUR: Jack Jacobs in Civil Engineering has done some consulting in Rhodesia. He says it's a smug enclave of white supremacists which can't last more than a few years.

PORTER: More power to Chris for getting out.

(CHRIS *appears, now dressed more casually.*)

CHRIS: Am I intruding?

SEYMOUR: Make yourself at home. *(He goes quickly.)*

CHRIS: That man doesn't like me.

PORTER: Give him a chance.

CHRIS: If he gives me one... But good news, Horatio! Your dear wife, I'm sure, will be pleased to hear that I've found a place to live.

PORTER: Where?

CHRIS: In the graduate student dormitory.

PORTER: Isn't that against the rules? For faculty to live in student housing?

CHRIS: Ah, but I'm not faculty, am I, being so temporary. I've even applied for the student rate on meals.

PORTER: Good luck.

CHRIS: On the other hand, I've been very distressed about my office situation. They asked me to share my space with one Natalie Katz.

PORTER: She'll be easy.

CHRIS: Too easy. She spends half the day on the telephone with her mother. How can I possibly hold conferences with my students with Madam Katz chattering aimlessly at the next desk?

PORTER: I guess all other office space is taken.

CHRIS: Not at all. There is a lovely, empty office on the fourth floor, overlooking the river.

PORTER: That's reserved for visiting dignitaries. Aldous Huxley was there. And Stephen Hawkings.

CHRIS: Ah, but no such luminaries are scheduled for this semester, are they? Which I pointed out to the gorgon who keeps the keys.

PORTER: Gorgon? Margie Ryan?

CHRIS: She was extremely disagreeable about even showing it to me.

PORTER: Margie? Disagreeable?

CHRIS: I suppose, like most secretaries, she expects me to take her to bed.

PORTER: Come on, Chris. She's happily married.

CHRIS: No matter. I made my case to the Dean, who said I could move in immediately.

PORTER: The Dean must like you.

CHRIS: I believe he may.

(A STUDENT *appears in the "doorway"* —*female this time.*)

STUDENT: May I speak to Professor Simpson, please?

CHRIS: Come in, Debbie.

STUDENT: I just wanted to say I've reserved Room 202 in Building 109 for eight thirty-five P M.

CHRIS: Excellent.

STUDENT: The Scheduling Office thought it was too large a room just for one section of The Old One-Two. But I said lots of people would show up.

CHRIS: As well they might, Debbie. If you post notices in the dormitories.

STUDENT: I did that, too.

CHRIS: Did you remember to underline that it's free?

STUDENT: Oh yes.

CHRIS: Well done, well done.

STUDENT: Thank you, sir.

CHRIS: Thank you who?

STUDENT: Thank you, Chris. *(She goes.)*

PORTER: What's that all about?

CHRIS: Tonight I'm showing *Lawrence of Arabia*.

PORTER: In the middle of Thucydides?

CHRIS: Exactly. It reflects back to the Warrior Ethic in Homer and forward to the Christian ideal of self-denial in the second semester.

PORTER: Hey. Good point.

CHRIS: You might want to send your own class. I'll be giving a short talk afterwards. *(Looks at his watch)* And speaking of the warrior ethic, it's time to resume battle on my meal tickets. Once more unto the breech... *(He goes.)*

PORTER: *(To audience)* And later I heard that over eighty students showed up and stayed for his lecture afterward...I would have gone myself, except that

Nancy had an evening class, so I had to stay home with the kids.

(PORTER goes off as ANITA and SEYMOUR enter, talking.)

SEYMOUR: Anita, *chère* colleague, no, no, no!

ANITA: Please, Seymour.

SEYMOUR: You can't suddenly take two separate sections and squeeze them together in the middle of the semester.

ANITA: Why not? Chris and I teach at the same time, in the same building.

SEYMOUR: Dear lady, our whole salvation lies in small classes.

ANITA: But this will be team-teaching. It's the latest thing.

SEYMOUR: It's the latest fad. Oh look, a class is a highly personal enterprise. During the semester, it takes on the special colors of its instructor. You should know that, more than most. You're one of the best we have.

ANITA: Tell that to the tenure committee.

SEYMOUR: I do every year.

ANITA: I'm beginning to lose my touch, Seymour. I practically had to teach *Antigone* in the nude in order to get a rise.

SEYMOUR: Remind me to sit in on your class.

ANITA: I'm losing confidence, Seymour.

SEYMOUR: Was this team-teaching Simpson's idea?

ANITA: Not really.

SEYMOUR: Sure it was. He's looking for a larger audience.

ANITA: He deserves one. I keep hearing him next door getting a hand.

ACT ONE

SEYMOUR: Probably from some cheap classroom theatrics... Are you sleeping with him, Anita?

ANITA: Of course not.

SEYMOUR: Do you want to?

ANITA: He happens to be gay.

SEYMOUR: You think so?

ANITA: He's certainly shown no sexual interest in me.

SEYMOUR: Then he's obviously gay as a goose.

ANITA: Thank you.

SEYMOUR: But whatever he is, he'd chew you alive if you taught with him. You'd end up sitting on the sidelines, taking notes like some graduate assistant.

ANITA: The Dean is thrilled with him, you know. He's gotten great student reports.

SEYMOUR: Is the Dean taking polls now?

ANITA: Students come and tell him. He says it's better having them get excited about Chris than picket the Rocket Research Lab. In fact, he's looking for a way to keep him around.

SEYMOUR: I have two words to say to that, Anita: Hughes Mearns.

ANITA: I beg your pardon.

SEYMOUR: *(Pronouncing it carefully)* Hughes Mearns. He was a late nineteenth-century English author, famous for one poem. May I recite it to you?

ANITA: If you have to.

SEYMOUR: "As I was going up the stair,
I met a man who wasn't there.
He wasn't there again today.
I wish, I wish he'd go away."

(ANITA *looks at* SEYMOUR *blankly.*)

SEYMOUR: Never mind. Let's go to the staff meeting. I've asked John Finley from Harvard to help us with Plato.

ANITA: I'll bet Chris stays. And I hope he does!

(ANITA *and* SEYMOUR *go off together.*)

(*Christmas music.* NANCY *comes on, in nightgown and bathrobe, carrying a chair. She sits as if at a dressing table and brushes her hair.*)

(PORTER *enters.*)

PORTER: *(Kissing the top of her head)* Great dinner, darling.

NANCY: We try.

PORTER: Yorkshire pudding yet.

NANCY: Which you should know is almost pure fat.

PORTER: Chris appreciated it.

NANCY: What's going on downstairs?

PORTER: The stockings are hung by the chimney with care. Chris is finishing up the dishes. The kids agreed to go to bed which gave me the chance to organize their presents under the tree. Hey, but wasn't it a great Christmas Eve? The way Chris got them off the telephone, and away from the T V, and made them listen to those glorious passages from the New Testament.

NANCY: They sat quietly, I'll say that.

PORTER: God, he read well. He gave the old story a new meaning. The exhausted Roman empire, obsessed with taxes. The whole world aching for a new way to live. And then the angel, the star in the East, the wise men, and lo and behold!

NANCY: Save it for Sunday. O K?

ACT ONE

PORTER: What about Chris's piano-playing? No one's touched that piano since Betsy quit her lessons. So he sits down, opens it up, and swings into those glorious old carols! And got the kids to sing along. In harmony!

NANCY: Oh that's what that was. Harmony.

PORTER: What's eating you, sweetheart?

NANCY: Have we got him all day tomorrow?

PORTER: Actually no. He wants to go into town to hear Handel's *Messiah* at Trinity Church in Copley Square.

NANCY: Good.

PORTER: Now why say that? Right after he gives you the complete recording of *Cosí Fan Tutti*.

NANCY: I'm beginning to like opera.

PORTER: But you don't like him?

NANCY: You're putting too much on him, Porter.

PORTER: What do you mean?

NANCY: Unto us a Savior is born.

PORTER: Oh come off it.

NANCY: He's just a man, Porter.

PORTER: Whatever that means.

NANCY: It means I'm glad he's going back to England next semester.

PORTER: Actually he's not.

NANCY: Not?

PORTER: Jack Appleman got a medical leave for his alcoholism, so the Dean asked Chris to teach Jack's section of The Old One-Two.

NANCY: I'll bet he leapt at the chance.

PORTER: He did not. He said he'd only do it if he could also teach his own course. So the Dean agreed. And Chris agreed to stay.

NANCY: That's the worst news I've heard since Nixon was reelected.

PORTER: That's not even funny.

NANCY: Let's go to bed, Porter. *(Starting out)* Aren't you coming?

PORTER: Not yet.

NANCY: It's Christmas Eve, sweetheart.

PORTER: Chris asked me to share a glass of port with him by the fire. He wants to pick my brains about the Department. I'll be up in a while.

NANCY: I'll be asleep. *(She goes off.)*

(Music: God Rest Ye, Merry Gentlemen*)*

(Light change. SEYMOUR *comes on.)*

SEYMOUR: How was your Christmas?

PORTER: *(As if coming to work)* Christmas Eve was glorious. As soon as Chris left, it was downhill. We had this huge family screamer about whether the kids could see *The Exorcist* on Christmas Day.

SEYMOUR: Why not?

PORTER: A movie? About Satanic possession? On a day dedicated to peace and love?

SEYMOUR: Sounds like they're crashing into adolescence.

PORTER: All I know is the whole house smells of Clearasil and foot deodorant.

SEYMOUR: Get any work done on your book?

PORTER: I'm thinking of changing the title.

ACT ONE

SEYMOUR: From...wait...*The Neglected Sector: The Family in American Fiction?*

PORTER: How about *The Dejected Sector: The Fiction of the American Family.*

SEYMOUR: The Dean asked about it again.

PORTER: Thank God for tenure. They can hassle me, but they can't fire me.

SEYMOUR: They can destroy you. They can force you to sit on the Athletic Committee and collect for the United Fund. They can keep you teaching nothing but introductory courses, year after year. And then they can give you the coup de grace of early retirement, coupled with slow starvation based on a minimal pension.

PORTER: I'll finish the book this summer, Seymour.

SEYMOUR: Please do. *(Taking out neat, handwritten sheet of paper)* Speaking of titles, how's this? *(Reading)* "Workshop on Will."

PORTER: What's that?

SEYMOUR: Your buddy-pal's new elective..."Workshop on Will." *(Reads from the document)* "Readings and performances of a number of Shakespeare's plays."

PORTER: Performances?

SEYMOUR: He plans to put things on. In direct competition with old Bill Everett's Drama Society. Poor Bill's colitis has flared up.

PORTER: Sorry to hear that.

SEYMOUR: Of course, your friend offers academic credit, which Bill doesn't.

PORTER: Chris didn't tell me.

SEYMOUR: Nor me. But he told the Dean. And apparently a student petition prepared the way.

(A STUDENT passes them.)

SEYMOUR: But enough of this bantering in the halls. Where can we talk seriously?

PORTER: Come into my office.

SEYMOUR: If your Rhodesian pal hasn't bugged it.

(PORTER and SEYMOUR move into PORTER's office.)

PORTER: Quit badmouthing him, Seymour.

SEYMOUR: He knew Bob Perlmutter got a Guggenheim even before Bob did.

PORTER: Bob got a Guggenheim?

SEYMOUR: For next fall. Which leaves a regular slot open. Guess who immediately applied to fill it. But can't, thank God, without a green card.

PORTER: Can't he get one?

SEYMOUR: Heh heh. Only if the head of the course he teaches—namely, *moi*—writes the immigration people that he is uniquely qualified.

PORTER: And you won't write that?

SEYMOUR: It would be a lie.

PORTER: Have a heart, man.

SEYMOUR: I do. For the hundreds of qualified young American PhDs now waiting tables in Central Square.

PORTER: Chris says that his master's degree from Oxford is superior to the American PhD.

SEYMOUR: The English always say that, but it's not true. We're way ahead of them in many areas.

PORTER: Not in Shakespeare.

CHRIS: We've got Shakespeare well covered by Jeff Feinstein, who's written two good books to prove it. So I'm afraid that after this term, your friend will have to return to Eton. Or Oxford. Or Rhodesia.

ACT ONE

(ANITA pokes her head in.)

ANITA: Good news! Chris Simpson has forty-three students registered for his special elective, "Workshop on Will"!

SEYMOUR: Now the war is winding down, and the draft is on hold, they can stop rioting and play Shakespeare.

ANITA: But forty-three warm bodies! For a course not even listed in the catalogue! He scattered a few mimeographed syllabi around the campus and caught forty-three fish.

SEYMOUR: Fred Nagler only got four for his course on the Reformation.

PORTER: That's a great course.

SEYMOUR: Fred has to cancel it. Four isn't enough, under the new budget.

ANITA: Yes, but Chris is upping our statistics by hauling in forty-three!

PORTER: How does he do it?

SEYMOUR: *(Producing another document)* Look at his syllabus and you'll see. *(He shows it around.)* He asks students to buy only six plays of Shakespeare, in the Pelican edition, at ninety cents a copy... That's a total of five dollars and forty cents, plus tax. Whereas most of our electives cost at least ten times that.

ANITA: No.

SEYMOUR: Add up the cost of your books some time. We never look, because we get our copies free. ... Furthermore, he calls for no quizzes, papers, or final exam. *(Reads)* "The course will meet Tuesday evenings, seven to ten P M in the Student Union lounge and be graded on Pass/Fail basis." ...See? Cheap, convenient, comfortable, and easy. Gresham's law: bad money drives out the good. Christopher Simpson drives out Fred Nagler.

PORTER: Where do they plan to perform?

ANITA: Everywhere. In his classes, in other classes...

SEYMOUR: Not in my classes...

ANITA: ...on the Great Lawn when the weather's warmer, in downtown Boston during lunch hour. And this morning he had a meeting with the President...

PORTER: Nixon?

ANITA: Our President here, silly. And Chris proposed that his class perform scenes from *As You Like It* at the annual Trustees meeting in May. And apparently the President said it was just the kind of hands-on cultural activity we in the Humanities should all be doing.

SEYMOUR: Is this the promised end, or image of that horror?

ANITA: I think it's exciting.

SEYMOUR: Exciting, Anita? Exciting? You find it exciting that these bright, half-educated kids, fresh from winning first prize at their high school science fairs, who will determine the shape of the next century, are now being officially encouraged to prance around town in baggy tights reciting lines they don't even understand?

ANITA: They'll learn more about Shakespeare being in his plays, than they ever will, churning out some dumb term paper comparing Cordelia to Antigone.

PORTER: Who assigns topics like that?

SEYMOUR: I do. And I get some first-rate essays.

PORTER: There is much to be said on both sides.

ACT ONE

SEYMOUR: There's nothing to be said on his. What suckers we are! What Philistines! We think it's culture personified whenever we hear an English accent.

PORTER: Chris is from Rhodesia.

SEYMOUR: Then his accent's fake, which makes it all the worse. Good Lord, what was the American Revolution all about? I thought we threw all that hoity-toity crap into Boston Harbor. I thought we were beginning to achieve some cultural confidence of our own. Yet whenever, wherever someone shows up with that fawncy way of talking—in the theater, the movies, or at some State Street Bank reception desk—we start genuflecting like peasants.

PORTER: Come on, Seymour. Shakespeare transcends all that.

SEYMOUR: Shakespeare is Shakespeare. And we should do him justice when we can. But there's more to the human experience than Shakespeare. And there's more to culture than an English accent.

ANITA: You obviously hate the English.

PORTER: Except he has an English wife.

SEYMOUR: I married my wife for more than her accent, sir.

ANITA: All I know is that Chris is onto something. Next year I'm cancelling my elective on Keats, and offering a poetry lab instead.

SEYMOUR: On what?

ANITA: Ourselves, Seymour. Ourselves. We'll write our own poems and read them in class.

SEYMOUR: Will you still be teaching The Old One-Two?

ANITA: I don't know. I'm getting tired of those old books.

SEYMOUR: Then we'll find others, Anita. Surely there are works which we all can agree to teach. A common curriculum—that's what we've got to hold onto. Good books that we can talk about among ourselves. And that we can get the students to talk about among *them*selves. So that we can build some basic sense of the human community between all of us. Then when they're designing a building or a bomb, maybe they'll remember the human dimension, and plan accordingly. Come on, Anita. Stay with us.

ANITA: I'll have to think about it.

SEYMOUR: *(With a sigh)* See, Porter? See what you've done by admitting that snake into our earthly paradise? Thank God he'll be gone by June. *(Glancing at* ANITA*)* Though I fear his effects will linger for some time after. *(Starts out, then stops)* You're welcome to talk about me when I'm gone. *(He goes.)*

PORTER: He's got Chris wrong.

ANITA: I couldn't agree more. Chris is full of ideas. You should have heard him the other night.

PORTER: What other night?

ANITA: He had us all over to his room for a little get-together.

PORTER: He didn't invite me.

ANITA: This was just junior faculty. Folks without... *(Mock reverence)* Ten-ure. If you'll pardon the expression. We found we could talk much more freely without people there who will be voting on our future.

PORTER: And did you?

ANITA: We certainly did. We talked about The Old One-Two. We said how tough it was to teach books outside our field, when we're trying to survive professionally.

ACT ONE

PORTER: That's true.

ANITA: So, Chris suggested... *(Looks at her watch)* But I've got to teach. *(Starts out)*

PORTER: Hey. What did he suggest?

ANITA: Oh lots of exciting things. Of course by then he had brought out some really good grass! *(She goes.)*

PORTER: *(Gathering up his books; to audience)* ...And so we embarked on the Judeo-Christian alternative... *(He starts off, as if to class.)*

(A female STUDENT approaches PORTER.)

STUDENT: Professor Platt. I want to transfer into your section.

PORTER: From whose?

STUDENT: Professor Simpson's.

PORTER: Am I that good?

STUDENT: It's not that.

PORTER: I hope he's not that bad.

STUDENT: He's wonderful!

PORTER: Then...?

STUDENT: I think I'm in love with him. *(She bursts into tears.)*

PORTER: Oh boy.

STUDENT: Last term when he was teaching us the *Aeneid*, I felt like Dido, the Queen of Carthage, who killed herself for love, thus starting the Pubic Wars.

PORTER: Punic. Punic Wars.

STUDENT: Whatever. But I've got to get out of his class.

PORTER: Have you shared these thoughts with Professor Simpson?

STUDENT: Of course. He said he could deal with it if we stayed in the Bible, but since we were about to move into the *Confessions of Saint Augustine*, he'd find me somewhat distracting.

PORTER: He has a point.

STUDENT: So he suggested I switch to you.

PORTER: How do I know you won't fall in love with me?

STUDENT: Oh don't worry about that. He said you were the tame type.

PORTER: Thank him for me.

STUDENT: I'll just sit quietly in back, and take notes, and pretend that human feelings have nothing to do with anything. *(She starts sobbing again.)*

PORTER: Oh hey... *(He touches her arm.)*

STUDENT: *(Jumping up)* Don't! Touch me again, and I'll report you to the Dean of Women! *(She hurries off, sobbing.)*

(Music. Bird sounds, leafy light. CHRIS *comes on in clean khaki trousers, an open shirt, carrying his little BOAC bag, along with other gear.)*

CHRIS: You're good to take me in again. Once the term ended, the ogress in charge of the dormitory literally locked me out of my room.

PORTER: You're always welcome here, Chris.

CHRIS: I brought *The Marriage of Figaro* to propitiate your lovely wife.

PORTER: She likes opera now, thanks to you.

CHRIS: I won't be able to listen to this one with her. If I may tuck my few paltry possessions under some bed, I plan to take a Grand Tour of America the Beautiful before I am obliged to return to whence I came.

ACT ONE

PORTER: Rhodesia?

CHRIS: England, of course.

PORTER: Will you be glad to get back?

CHRIS: No.

PORTER: Why not?

CHRIS: England's too small.

PORTER: I hope you don't find America too big.

CHRIS: That's what I like about it.

PORTER: How will you get around?

CHRIS: *(With an awkward hitchhiking gesture)* Ah. The key to this kingdom lies in the humble thumb.

PORTER: I'll give you the names of some folks to look up along the way.

CHRIS: You are most kind… Meanwhile, I'll "stow my gear," as Conrad says in *The Secret Sharer*. *(He takes up his gear and goes.)*

PORTER: *(To audience)* I dropped him off at an entrance ramp to the Massachusetts Turnpike, with his distinguished thumb pointing politely to California. Even as I drove away, I could see in my rearview mirror an old Volkswagen microbus, loaded with multi-racial musicians, stopping to pick him up. *(He goes to his office.)* So Nancy went to summer school, the kids got summer jobs, and I used the summer to write my book. *(Settles in at his desk; writes)*

(NANCY *comes on, carrying a stack of postcards.)*

NANCY: A postcard from Chris.

(CHRIS's *voice is heard over speakers.)*

CHRIS: "O Mighty Cataract and Gorge…"

PORTER: *(At his desk; to audience)* Niagara Falls.

NANCY: *(Another card)* Another from Toledo…

PORTER: *(To audience)* Where he stayed with my parents.

CHRIS: Enjoyed your mother.

PORTER: *(To audience)* My father didn't like him.

NANCY: *(A piece of paper)* A bill from the emergency room at the Minneapolis General Hospital…

CHRIS: *(Weakly)* Strep throat… Please pay…

NANCY: This one's from Los Angeles.

CHRIS: "…like stout Cortez, when with eagle eyes He stared at the Pacific…?"

NANCY: I thought Balboa discovered the Pacific.

PORTER: Well now Chris has.

NANCY: *(Flipping through more cards)* San Diego, the Grand Canyon, Santa Fe, New Orleans, Nashville, Washington, D C…? The Lincoln Memorial…

CHRIS: "We've stood upon Achilles' tomb
And heard Troy doubted; time will doubt of Rome…?"

PORTER: *(To audience)* Sounds like Byron.

NANCY: Yes, but who's that "we"?

PORTER: That's the poetic "we."

NANCY: Is it? I wonder…

CHRIS: Arrive back Labor Day.

PORTER: Uh-oh. No one will be here. We're visiting the Parkers on the Cape.

NANCY: Oh he has a key.

PORTER: Since when?

NANCY: Oh I don't know. For quite a while…? *(She goes off.)*

PORTER: *(Looks after her; then gathers up his papers)* And I got Margie Ryan to type up a draft of my book.

ACT ONE

(Music. CHRIS *comes on, in jeans, plaid shirt, possibly cowboy boots and hat. He carries a black, bound manuscript.)*

CHRIS: Porter!

*(*CHRIS *greets* PORTER *enthusiastically.)*

CHRIS: I assume you left your manuscript on my bed because you wanted me to read it while you frolicked on the beaches of Cape Cod.

PORTER: Did you like it?

CHRIS: I see you persuaded Madam Ryan to type it.

PORTER: How did you know?

CHRIS: The unusual amount of typographical errors. I noted them in the margins. *(Hands him the book)*

PORTER: What about the ideas?

CHRIS: Ideas?

PORTER: My thoughts. About the American family. What do you think?

CHRIS: Oh fine. Interesting. If true. *(Glances at watch)* But I have an appointment in town. *(Starting off)*

PORTER: I'd love more feedback, Chris. Before you go back to England.

CHRIS: Ah, but I might stay.

PORTER: Without a green card?

CHRIS: There are more things in heaven and earth, Horatio, than are dreamt of in your philosophy.

*(*CHRIS *goes as lights change.* SEYMOUR *comes on.)*

PORTER: *(Still holding the manuscript)* You left this on my desk.

SEYMOUR: I did.

PORTER: Did you read it?

SEYMOUR: Immediately.

PORTER: What do you think?

SEYMOUR: Let's go into your office, Porter.

(PORTER *and* SEYMOUR *go in.*)

SEYMOUR: You've written a bad book, Porter.

PORTER: I guess there are a lot of typos.

SEYMOUR: The typing's fine, the thinking's terrible.

PORTER: How do you mean?

SEYMOUR: All the way through, you confuse the idea of gentility with the idea of civility. Genteel is just manners and pretension, sticking your pinkie out when you drink your tea. A civil society is much, much more. It deals with faith and trust and mutual respect. Look, I'm being rude as hell to you right now, but I'm also being civilized, because you and I trust each other enough to deal with an unpleasant truth.

PORTER: Seymour—

SEYMOUR: *(Handing it back)* I wish I could tell you how to revise it, but I can't, because there's nothing there, and nothing will come of nothing, as the poet says. You'll have to start again.

PORTER: *(Examining it)* You've spilled coffee on it.

SEYMOUR: Sorry. My kids jumped into my lap.

PORTER: *(Coldly)* Thanks for taking the time.

SEYMOUR: Hey, they're showing *Duck Soup* in Kenmore Square. Let's go see the Marx Brothers break up one of Margaret Dumont's genteel parties.

PORTER: I've got to prepare a class.

SEYMOUR: You do not.

PORTER: I do. I don't just wing it, like some guys I know. I study. I make notes. I prepare!

ACT ONE

SEYMOUR: *(Putting his arm around him)* Porter, Porter, Porter.

(ANITA comes in.)

ANITA: Special meeting in the Dean's office. Subject: Christopher Simpson.

SEYMOUR: He's over the Atlantic, even as we speak.

ANITA: He's over in the Dean's office, asking to stay.

SEYMOUR: He doesn't have a green card.

ANITA: He doesn't need one. He just married an American. *(She goes.)*

SEYMOUR: I need the Marx Brothers immediately. *(He goes.)*

PORTER: *(To audience)* And soon the halls were buzzing.

(Lights change. NANCY *comes on, wiping her hands on a dishtowel.)*

NANCY: So? Tell me.

PORTER: *(Joining her)* He met her in California.

NANCY: That "we" on the postcard. Remember?

PORTER: Her name is Barbara Birdfeather.

NANCY: Birdfeather?

PORTER: She's part Apache.

NANCY: Can't get more American than that.

PORTER: They were married down at City Hall. The day his divorce came through.

NANCY: Divorce?

PORTER: He was married before in England.

NANCY: And he never told you any of this?

PORTER: Nope.

NANCY: You should pin him down some time, Porter.

PORTER: Pin him down?

NANCY: You never ask him things.

PORTER: What things?

NANCY: I don't know. Things that friends ask. What's the scoop on this former wife? Do you have a family? Where are you heading? Stuff like that.

PORTER: *(Cringing)* I couldn't, Nancy.

NANCY: Why the hell not?

PORTER: It would be rude and intrusive. The English are a very private people.

NANCY: I think you're scared.

PORTER: Scared of what?

NANCY: Scared he'll say bug off, or out of my way, or something.

(Telephone rings; PORTER *"answers".)*

PORTER: Hello.

(SEYMOUR *appears somewhere in a light. He might be holding a drink.)*

SEYMOUR: *(As if on telephone)* Can we talk?

PORTER: *(To* NANCY*)* Seymour wants to talk.

NANCY: Now there's a friend. Or do you think he's being rude and intrusive. *(She goes.)*

SEYMOUR: The junior faculty just met with the Dean.

PORTER: About what?

SEYMOUR: Me. They accused me of being inflexible about The Old One-Two.

PORTER: You are, of course.

SEYMOUR: They want your friend to take it over.

PORTER: What?

ACT ONE

SEYMOUR: But he said No.

PORTER: No?

SEYMOUR: He said his position here was too precarious. So the Dean handed him a regular, tenure-track position.

PORTER: Then and there?

SEYMOUR: He likes him. The President likes him. So does the Board of Trustees, after sitting through those sappy scenes from *As You Fucking Like It*.

PORTER: So then Chris said Yes?

SEYMOUR: Not at all.

PORTER: Out of loyalty to you?

SEYMOUR: Out of loyalty to his quote younger colleagues unquote. He said he couldn't possibly run a course which the junior faculty found so restrictive. So the Dean said open it up.

PORTER: Open it up?

SEYMOUR: People can teach whatever they want. Chris quoted Mao: "Let a hundred flowers grow".

PORTER: Oh boy.

SEYMOUR: We are all now on our own. *(His voice breaks; he turns upstage, takes out a handkerchief.)*

PORTER: Seymour? *(No answer)* Are you all right? *(No answer)* Seymour? Are you there?

SEYMOUR: *(Wiping his eyes)* I'm here.

PORTER: It's just a course, Seymour.

SEYMOUR: That's what Caesar said when he burned the library at Alexandria. Just a building.

PORTER: Did Caesar really say that?

SEYMOUR: No.

PORTER: Look. I'll call Chris in the morning. I'll say that here in America, we don't cater to this kind of bald careerism.

SEYMOUR: We don't?

(NANCY *comes on, beckons, goes off.*)

PORTER: Got to go, buddy. Dinner's on the table.

SEYMOUR: *(Glancing off)* Ditto here...He has no children.

PORTER: What's that from?

SEYMOUR: MacDuff says it about Macbeth.

PORTER: Yeah, yeah.

SEYMOUR: No, really. He does. *(He goes.)*

(Lights change.)

PORTER: *(To audience)* So the next morning...

(CHRIS *comes hurriedly down a "corridor".*)

PORTER: Got a minute, Chris?

CHRIS: Sorry. I have a command performance in half an hour.

PORTER: Command performance?

(*A* STUDENT *comes on wearing wrinkly tights and a silly Elizabethan costume.*)

CHRIS: We're doing some scenes for Earth Day on the steps of the state capitol. Senator Edward Kennedy will be there. *(To* STUDENT*)* Your doublet needs fixing. Here's an empty classroom.

(CHRIS *leads the* STUDENT *into a lighted area, fusses with his costume.*)

PORTER: *(Following him)* You owe Seymour an apology, Chris.

(*A female* STUDENT *comes on in an equally tacky costume.*)

STUDENT: Chris, can you fix this sleeve?

ACT ONE

CHRIS: *(As he fusses with the costumes)* Apology? For what?

PORTER: Commandeering his course.

CHRIS: You mean, improving the curriculum. *(To* STUDENTS*)* Don't mind us. Rehearse your lines.

(The STUDENTS *start rehearsing. We can't hear always what they are saying, but we see standard stereotyped gestures: the arm-waving, the kneeling, the bowing, the hand-kissing.)*

PORTER: You never cut me in on any of this.

CHRIS: *(Repositioning the* STUDENTS*)* Who are you? My Father Confessor?

STUDENTS: *(Absurd fragments seep through)* I'll wager a farthing, quoth she… No more than the Queen's cat can whistle at a toad… Nay, then the dolphin would out-stare the basilisk…

PORTER: I'm your friend, Chris. You stayed in my house, lived with my family, visited my parents. I've shared my thoughts with you all along, and you never even told me you were married.

CHRIS: I apologize. Apparently I have yet to acquire that strange American habit of spewing forth one's soul at the slightest opportunity.

STUDENTS: Prithee, love is a clyster-pipe when the cock crows seven…I'd rather card a sheep than lime a starling…

PORTER: O K, Chris. Forget the personal stuff. Let's talk business. If you want to change the course, call a meeting of everyone teaching it, and make your case. Then we all can vote on it.

CHRIS: We're late for our performance. *(To* STUDENTS*)* On ward and upward, people.
Come, players, let's away.

(The STUDENTS *laugh and start out.)*

PORTER: *(Grabbing* CHRIS's *arm)* I'm serious, Chris.

CHRIS: Oh for God's sake, Porter, stop stage-managing other people's lives and start living your own! *(He shakes loose and joins his* STUDENTS.*)* Come, players, let's away, A Kennedy calls, and we must not say nay!

(CHRIS *and the* STUDENTS *sweep off.* PORTER *remains, shocked.)*

PORTER: *(To audience)* That did it, of course. *(Shouting toward where* CHRIS *has gone)* THAT DID IT, YOU FUCKING LIMEY BASTARD! From here on in, it's a very different ballgame! *(To audience)* And if any of you has ever taken The Old One-Two, I'm sure I would have reminded you of Achilles in the *Iliad* brooding in his tent...or Cain in the *Bible,* smoldering with envy... or Satan, the deepest, darkest circle of Dante's *Inferno,* plotting some terrible revenge!

(Strident, revolutionary music comes up. Quick blackout)

END OF ACT ONE

ACT TWO

(Music)

(PORTER *is at his desk, reading a book, jotting down lecture notes. A brown paper bag beside him indicates he's had lunch. After a moment,* SEYMOUR *comes in.)*

SEYMOUR: *(Holding a note)* You say to stop by after class.

PORTER: Oh right. *(Reaches into his brown bag, holds out his apple)* I wondered if you wanted my apple.

SEYMOUR: As Eve said to Adam.

PORTER: Do you?

SEYMOUR: No thanks.

PORTER: *(Taking a bite of it)* Thank God. That was just a lame excuse to have lunch with somebody. Have a seat.

SEYMOUR: *(Settling in; eating his own lunch)* Remember in Faulkner's *Light in August*? When people stop eating together, the community disintegrates.

PORTER: It's true. At this time last year, we'd all be at the round table in the cafeteria, figuring out how to teach Plato's *Symposium*.

SEYMOUR: Gone are the days.

(PORTER *and* SEYMOUR *eat.)*

PORTER: I keep wondering why I brought him in.

SEYMOUR: Don't bother.

PORTER: Maybe I'm subconsciously anti-Semitic.

SEYMOUR: *(As he eats)* That could be it.

PORTER: You think I am?

SEYMOUR: Of course.

PORTER: I don't mean anti-Semitic. I just mean, well, all right, anti-Semitic. You think I am?

SEYMOUR: I do.

PORTER: No I mean seriously. Maybe I subconsciously felt the Jewish community was over-represented here.

SEYMOUR: That's it, in a nutshell.

PORTER: Seriously. That's a possibility. Sometimes I feel that everyone is Jewish, except me.

SEYMOUR: Everybody is.

PORTER: You, and Bob Perlmutter, and Natalie Katz. It seems you all went to the same high school, and played the violin, and used words like "mensch" and "schlock" and "putz" and "goy". That's what I feel like, sometimes. A goy.

SEYMOUR: That's what you are.

PORTER: Yeah, well, maybe that's why I brought him in. There he was, standing in the doorway, with his English accent and his Oxford gray suit and regimental tie, and I must've thought, "Well whadya know? A kindred spirit. Welcome to Yeshiva-on-the-Charles!"

SEYMOUR: Except that he's Jewish, too.

PORTER: How can you tell?

SEYMOUR: It takes one to know one. The push, the hustle, the drive for the top. Typically Jewish behavior. He's changed his name from Sammy Glick.

PORTER: Oh Jesus.

SEYMOUR: Jesus is Jewish.

ACT TWO   51

PORTER: Stop. I hear you, Seymour. I categorize people too much, don't I? I stretch them out on the Procrustean Bed of ethnic identity.

SEYMOUR: You do...

PORTER: Sure I do. I frame people in these phony intellectual categories. I forget to look at the concrete person. I did it to Chris, I do it to you. It's all a head trip. That's what academic life has done to me.

SEYMOUR: How'd you get into this weird kind of work, anyway? You've never really told me.

PORTER: I've never really wanted to... After college, I worked for Houghton-Mifflin. Editing, getting nowhere. Then Nancy got pregnant with our first, so I took a loan and went for my PhD. As insurance. My old man knew some professor of engineering. Got me an interview. Taught The Old One-Two, grunted out a book, one thing led to another. See? It wasn't a real choice. I kind of fell into it.

SEYMOUR: Do you like it?

PORTER: Who really likes what they do?

SEYMOUR: I do. Very much.

PORTER: Right. I'm beginning to see that now...Hey Seymour, I really apologize for bringing Chris in. I'll try to look at folks differently, so it won't happen again.

SEYMOUR: Here's what I think. If Christopher Simpson hadn't shown up, we would have had to invent him. Americans have always been suckers for the English thing. Look at the Duke and the Dolphin in *Huck Finn*, using Shakespeare to bamboozle the poor rubes. Look at our public television. A good half of its programming celebrates the English class system. I suppose it all boils down to some kind of nostalgic guilt for the mother country we rebelled against. And we Jews are the worst offenders. *(He gets up; starts out.)*

PORTER: Where are you going?

SEYMOUR: Over to Newbury Street to meet my English wife. We plan to buy a London Fog raincoat and a Laura Ashley bedspread, before we catch Maggie Smith playing Noel Coward at the Colonial Theatre.

PORTER: I'll walk you out.

(PORTER *and* SEYMOUR *walk.*)

SEYMOUR: How's the family?

PORTER: The same. The evening meal has gone totally by the boards. Despite the new kitchen, the kids won't eat with us, or if they do, they won't eat the same thing.

SEYMOUR: And Nancy?

PORTER: Since she can't feed them, she's working on feeding the world. Right now she's writing a joint report with a Nigerian exchange student on alternative foods for emerging cultures. They're calling it, "Our Friend the Pumpkin."

SEYMOUR: How about your own work?

PORTER: I'm changing the title again. I might just call it *The Anti-Semite at Home Alone.*

SEYMOUR: Maybe you should get back to that novel.

PORTER: Wish I could.

(SEYMOUR *goes.*)

(NANCY *comes on, bundled up, carrying a tote bag.*)

NANCY: I'm off. There's a chicken pot pie in the microwave. Don't forget to rotate. The kids have already eaten... Oh, and Chris called.

PORTER: That bastard.

ACT TWO

NANCY: He seemed very sweet, actually.

PORTER: That's because he's in command now.

NANCY: He wants to know what you plan to teach next semester.

PORTER: Nothing under him, that's for sure. I've got my Fitzgerald elective and I'll figure out something else.

NANCY: *(Kissing him briskly)* Well, I'm late for my class.

PORTER: When will you be back?

NANCY: Quite late, actually. I'll probably have coffee afterwards.

PORTER: With your third-world buddy?

NANCY: Probably.

PORTER: Maybe that's why you're having trouble sleeping.

NANCY: Because of him?

PORTER: Because of the coffee.

NANCY: Maybe. *(She goes.)*

(Light change. STUDENTS *set up a couple of large pillows.* ANITA *comes on, carrying a tray with a bottle and two glasses.)*

ANITA: How about some sherry, Porter? Chris gave me a bottle for my birthday.

PORTER: *(Joining her)* Thanks.

*(*ANITA *and* PORTER *settle on the pillows.)*

ANITA: *(Pouring)* I don't normally hold meetings in my apartment, Porter. But unlike my male counterparts, I have to be home when my children get out of school.

PORTER: Nice place.

ANITA: Tiny. *(Indicating off)* The bedroom is nothing but bed. *(Sipping sherry)* Now. What gives? I found your rather cryptic request on my desk.

PORTER: I'd like to teach a section of your writing course, Anita.

ANITA: You? Stuffy old Porter Platt? Teaching writing?

PORTER: As you may have heard, I'm having trouble getting into my book. Maybe I need a few stretch exercises.

ANITA: Don't we all.

PORTER: The Dean said your course had too many students.

ANITA: I do! It's a gas! They're clambering to get in, now that it fulfills a basic Humanities credit. We can all thank for Chris for that.

PORTER: I don't thank Chris for anything.

ANITA: You were such close friends.

PORTER: I can't teach under him. Leave it at that.

ANITA: But isn't this rather ridiculous? Me, a lowly lecturer, interviewing a tenured professor for a funky little course in creative writing. Why not just go ahead and teach it?

PORTER: Because the Dean says it's your course and you have the right to decide.

ANITA: Then I'd like to see a specimen.

PORTER: Of my urine?

ANITA: Of your writing, silly. I ask it of everyone involved. Including myself.

PORTER: My last article was published two years ago in *The Sewanee Review*. You can get it in the library.

ACT TWO

ANITA: Oh Porter. I'm not interested in your scholarly work. The title of this course is "Writing and the Self," remember? We will be searching for our own personal voice. Now here... *(She gets a pad and ballpoint pen.)* Write something. A paragraph, a sentence, maybe even just a phrase—which feels real and honest and true.

PORTER: Here? Now?

ANITA: Why not?

(PORTER takes the pen, starts to write, then stops.)

PORTER: I can't. I feel too much under the gun.

ANITA: Don't be silly.

PORTER: *(Tries again; stops)* Nope. Still can't. As Byron says, "The caged eagle cannot mate."

(Pause)

ANITA: You feel caged, Porter?

PORTER: Maybe tonight when I get home...

ANITA: You still won't be able to do it.

PORTER: Why do you say that?

ANITA: Because you're hung up, Porter Platt.

PORTER: Hung up?

ANITA: On something you don't dare deal with.

PORTER: And what might that be?

ANITA: Christopher Simpson.

(Pause)

PORTER: Go on.

ANITA: Do you want me to spell it out?

PORTER: Please do.

ANITA: I find this somewhat embarrassing.

PORTER: Are you by any chance saying...?

ANITA: I think I am.

PORTER: Oh Anita, for shit's sake! You're always running around saying everybody's gay.

ANITA: Lately it seems that everybody is.

PORTER: Well I'm not, thanks.

ANITA: You are certainly obsessed with the man.

PORTER: I'm pissed off at the man.

ANITA: You bent over backwards to get him in here.

PORTER: I'd bend over forwards to get him out.

ANITA: See? Gay.

PORTER: Oh shit.

ANITA: There's nothing wrong with being gay, Porter.

PORTER: Except that I'm not.

ANITA: *(A big sip of sherry)* Prove it.

PORTER: How do I prove a negative?

ANITA: By being positive.

PORTER: *(Getting up)* I'm outa here.

ANITA: *(Standing in his way)* You're walking away from it.

PORTER: Move, Anita!

ANITA: How can I possibly let you teach the Self when you're so out of touch with your own?

PORTER: *(Trying to push past her)* Let me pass, please, Anita.

ANITA: You've "passed" all your life, haven't you? Isn't it time to release?

PORTER: *(Grabbing her shoulders)* Release? Release? How? By kissing the guy? Like this? *(He kisses her angrily.)*

ACT TWO

ANITA: That was a very cold kiss, Porter.

PORTER: Oh it's warmth you want. How about this? *(Kisses her again)*

ANITA: Now you're angry.

PORTER: I've got to get back.

ANITA: I can't let you leave like this. *(Taking out a handkerchief)* At least let me wipe your fevered brow... *(She does; she wipes the inside of his collar.)* You are hot under the collar, aren't you?

PORTER: How'd you guess?

ANITA: Do you think anger is an aphrodisiac, Porter?

PORTER: Maybe.

ANITA: I do. I think that's why the Greeks had the God of War conjoin with the Goddess of Love... *(Putting her handkerchief away)* Now go, if you want.

PORTER: Give me another sherry, Anita...

ANITA: Say please.

PORTER: *(Takes her glass; downs it)* Now I want to see the rest of your apartment. *(Takes her toward the bedroom)*

ANITA: The bed isn't even made.

PORTER: *(Pulling her)* So much the better.

ANITA: Hey! I thought the caged eagle couldn't mate.

PORTER: Fuck the caged eagle.

(PORTER *pulls* ANITA *offstage.*)

(Blackout)

(Erotic music)

(Lights up. PORTER *comes on, buttoning his shirt.)*

PORTER: There.

(ANITA *comes on, buttoning her blouse.)*

ANITA: Whatever that means.

PORTER: How was that for self-expression, baby?

ANITA: I'd say it was fraught with ambiguity.

PORTER: Oh yes?

ANITA: Some people might even call it a rape.

PORTER: Oh yeah? Who raped whom, I'd like to know.

ANITA: I'll say this: If I weren't committed to pass/fail, I'd give it a C minus.

PORTER: At least I proved something.

ANITA: Whatever you proved, Porter, I won't take it to the Women's Grievance Committee if you don't bandy it about in the halls.

PORTER: It's a deal. *(He starts out.)*

ANITA: Wait, Porter. One thing.

(PORTER stops.)

ANITA: Please don't teach in my course. You'll just screw up your students, you're such a mess.

PORTER: So are you, Anita.

ANITA: I know I am. But at least I admit it.

(A buzzer sounds.)

ANITA: There are my kids. Scoot, lover. Out the back. *(She goes off, clearing the tray.)*

(A STUDENT clears the pillows.)

PORTER: *(To audience)* So for the spring semester, along with my elective, I taught English as a Second Language to Africans, Asians, and Pacific Islanders.

(Lights change.)

(SEYMOUR crosses the stage.)

SEYMOUR: Coming to the faculty meeting?

ACT TWO

PORTER: What faculty meeting?

SEYMOUR: Where have you been?

PORTER: Home, whenever I could be. The kids have been acting up.

SEYMOUR: It might interest you to know that this is a special meeting of the entire Institute faculty. To discuss the Humanities requirement.

(A STUDENT sets up a couple of folding chairs, as if in the back of an auditorium.)

PORTER: What's to discuss?

SEYMOUR: Everything. The whole department is up for grabs.

(SEYMOUR sits in a folding chair. ANITA comes on.)

ANITA: *(To SEYMOUR)* May I join you?

SEYMOUR: Why? Am I coming apart?

ANITA: *(Sitting)* Stop with the Groucho-isms, Seymour. This is serious. They want to get rid of our whole department.

SEYMOUR: Sit down, Porter.

PORTER: I'll stand, thanks. *(To audience)* You see, once Chris had broken up The Old One-Two, the entire curriculum came under fire. We were called vague and soft, taking valuable time from the hard sciences.

(Sound of applause)

PORTER: A Nobel-prize-winning astrophysicist accused us of... *(German accent)* force-feeding our students, like Strasbourg geese... We were wrong for these times, and wrong for this place, so polarized around science.

(More applause)

SEYMOUR: *(Low to ANITA)* Paralyzed around science.

ANITA: How true, how true.

PORTER: *(To audience)* Others took up the cry. A nuclear engineer, who had helped build the bomb at Los Alamos, pointed out that the fine young men who paid so much to come here, and who were so vulnerable to the draft, were surely old enough to design their own curriculum.

(More applause)

ANITA: *(To SEYMOUR)* This time next year, I'll probably be bussing trays at Legal Sea Food. You're lucky. You've got tenure.

SEYMOUR: Not if they disband the Department. We'll all disappear, like the whooping crane.

PORTER: *(To audience)* But then Chris Simpson rose to respond.

(A wooden podium, with a mike, appears; CHRIS comes up to it, to speak. He wears a sportcoat, shirt, and tie, along with immaculately laundered khakis.)

CHRIS: My name is Christopher Simpson, I teach the Humanities here, and I'd like to say a word in our defense.

PORTER: *(Whispering to SEYMOUR and ANITA)* How come he's speaking?

SEYMOUR: The Dean asked him to.

(The mike squeals.)

CHRIS: *(Tapping the mike)* Does this thing work? Can people hear me?

PORTER: *(To SEYMOUR)* The Dean should be speaking himself.

SEYMOUR: He felt it would be inappropriate. Seeing as how he's just accepted a job at Brown. Where they have no curriculum at all.

ACT TWO 61

CHRIS: *(To audience)* You can see... *(Tapping the dead mike)* ...that the gods are already demonstrating the limits of science and technology.

(Sounds of laughter. The mike begins to sputter again. CHRIS *calls off.)*

CHRIS: I notice several of my students standing in back. May I invite them to apply their expertise to this problem?

(Two STUDENTS *scurry out, begin to fuss with wires and connections.* CHRIS *comes to the side of the podium.)*

CHRIS: Meanwhile you'll have to put up with my still, small voice unamplified.

(The STUDENTS *continue to work at his feet.)*

CHRIS: I shall begin by calling your attention to... *(He continues to speak silently.)*

PORTER: *(To audience)* And once again, the English accent worked. He was Churchill defending his stalwart island, Alistair Cooke presenting Masterpiece Theatre, Sir Laurence Olivier pushing Polaroid cameras.

CHRIS: *(To audience)* And I should like to go on to say... *(More silent speech)*

PORTER: *(To audience)* He spoke of human history and the heritage of the past. He cited civilizations that failed because they lost that heritage. He went on to name names—in the English way...

CHRIS: *(To audience)* Eeschylus...? S'nt Augustine...Don Quix-ott...

PORTER: And he evoked others by including their full names...

CHRIS: Leonardo Da Vinci, Dante Alighieri, Alfred Lord Tennyson...

SEYMOUR: *(Low to* ANITA*)* Farrah Fawcett Majors.

ANITA: Sssshh.

PORTER: *(To audience)* And then came *Bartlett's Familiar Quotations*...

CHRIS: *(To audience)* "The still, sad music of humanity"..."Man is the measure of all things"..."The proper study of mankind is man"...

ANITA: *(Low to* SEYMOUR*)* Or woman, dammit...

SEYMOUR: *(Low to* ANITA*)* Now I know who stole the copy of Bartlett's from Department Headquarters.

CHRIS: *(To audience)* We all remember Lear's wrenching lines in Act Five, Scene Three, when he holds Cordelia's body in his arm...

PORTER: *(To audience; as* CHRIS *"talks" on)* And we all did. We remembered. Somehow he managed to include everyone in that vast auditorium into a privileged circle of educated men and women...

(A STUDENT *indicates to* CHRIS *the mike is repaired. He indicates that he prefers to continue without it, so the* STUDENTS *sit enraptured at his feet.)*

CHRIS: *(To audience)* ...And I suspect Descartes amuses you as much as he does me when he attempts to account rationally for the existence of God...

PORTER: *(To audience)* We all chuckled knowingly...

CHRIS: *(To audience)* But I'm sure that all of us raise an eyebrow whenever we read that strange chapter in the Gospel According to S'nt Matthew...

PORTER: *(To audience)* Oh sure. We knew that passage. Because by then we were, all of us, the most learned people in the world. We were...

ACT TWO

CHRIS: *(To audience)* Raphael's School of Athens, the French Academy, the Founding Fathers...? *(He takes up the repaired mike.)* The last, best hope of mankind!

(Ringing applause)

ANITA: *(Clapping; getting up)* Right on! Right on!

SEYMOUR: *(Getting up)* Oh hell. Why not? *(He applauds politely.)*

(CHRIS smiles and exits, with the two STUDENTS clapping him on the back.)

ANITA: *(To SEYMOUR)* Have you changed your mind about him?

SEYMOUR: Not at all. It was your typical Oxford Debating Society performance. Coupled with the sort of ham posturing you see at Stratford, Ontario, for the benefit of summering school teachers.

ANITA: But he saved the day! He kept us alive!

(They join PORTER.)

ANITA: What did you think of Chris's speech, Porter?

PORTER: I think it was terrific, goddammit to hell! *(He goes.)*

ANITA: *(Looking after him)* There is a relationship I simply don't understand.

SEYMOUR: We'd better go teach.

ANITA: Right. I keep forgetting that's what we're being paid for.

(ANITA goes off; a STUDENT stops SEYMOUR.)

STUDENT: May I speak to you, Professor Blum?

SEYMOUR: *(Checking his watch)* I've got five minutes.

STUDENT: You've ruined my life.

SEYMOUR: I've ruined so many, remind me how.

STUDENT: You gave me a bad recommendation.

SEYMOUR: To where?

STUDENT: The Royal Academy of Dramatic Art in London, England.

SEYMOUR: Ah yes.

STUDENT: Chris Simpson recommended me, but they asked for a second opinion, so I gave them your name. You taught me The Old One-Two my freshman year, and I thought you were a good man.

SEYMOUR: In that course, I was. Now they've got me teaching The Semiotics of Cinema, I've become quite evil.

STUDENT: Chris says you don't like him. So you took it out on me.

SEYMOUR: Not true. I made a point of going to his production of *Coriolanus* just so I could see your performance.

STUDENT: You must have written something terrible.

SEYMOUR: I simply wrote that you worked very hard to imitate an English accent, and kept your head when your toga fell off.

STUDENT: Why'd you put that in?

SEYMOUR: Because it was your most truthful moment. Though next time you might want to wear more substantial underclothes.

STUDENT: Very funny.

SEYMOUR: I also wrote that according to your thesis advisor in Chemistry, you were unusually gifted in the field of polymer semi-conductors and have already received a substantial job offer from General Electric upon graduation.

ACT TWO

STUDENT: I can't afford to fly over and audition. My parents are deep in hock for my four years here.

SEYMOUR: I'm late for my class.

STUDENT: *(Calling after him)* I'll have to take the job at G E, Professor. Thanks for ruining my life.

SEYMOUR: We help when we can.

(They exit either way.)

(Music. Light change to night.)

(A STUDENT puts out a coat-tree.)

(NANCY enters on tip-toe, in her overcoat, carrying her tote bag. She quietly takes off her coat and hangs it up. PORTER comes on, in a sweater.)

PORTER: *(Kissing her)* I was worried.

NANCY: I had a test.

PORTER: How did it go?

NANCY: I flunked.

PORTER: You always say that, and then pass with flying colors.

NANCY: This time I know.

PORTER: They've already graded it?

NANCY: I graded myself.

PORTER: You had a new kind of test tonight?

NANCY: I had an affair tonight.

(Pause)

PORTER: With your Nigerian gentleman?

NANCY: Yes.

PORTER: Why?

NANCY: Why? I don't know why. Maybe because things have been so rocky lately between you and me.

PORTER: Can't deny that.

NANCY: There he was, this young, attractive, sexy man, always turning around to smile at me in class, always asking me out for coffee afterwards.

PORTER: Working with you on the pumpkin project.

NANCY: All that. And tonight, after the coffee, he asked me to his apartment. He said his roommates weren't there. So I thought about it. And said Yes.

PORTER: That was the test?

NANCY: That was the test.

PORTER: How did you flunk?

NANCY: He put these African tunes on the stereo, which I didn't know how to dance to, and we smoked some pot, which just made me more self-conscious, and finally one of his roommates came back, and I grabbed my stuff and ran.

PORTER: So nothing happened.

NANCY: No. *(Pause)* I mean, yes.

PORTER: You went to bed with him?

NANCY: It didn't mean anything, Porter. I felt terrible the whole time—cheap and guilty and old.

PORTER: That's how you flunked?

NANCY: That's how I flunked.

PORTER: Hmm. *(Thinks; then magnanimously)* You passed, Nancy. In my book, you passed.

NANCY: You think?

PORTER: I do. And I admit I've been a lousy husband lately.

NANCY: We've both been bad.

PORTER: I've been worse. I want to tell you about what happened between me and Anita.

ACT TWO

NANCY: *(Interrupting)* It happened with Chris, too, you know.

PORTER: I wanted to teach in Anita's writing course, so I—

NANCY: *(Interrupting again)* I said it happened with Chris.

PORTER: *(Exploding)* WHAT?

NANCY: Here we go.

PORTER: What the fuck did you do with Chris?

NANCY: Calm down.

PORTER: In this house?

NANCY: Sssh. The kids.

PORTER: In my home?

NANCY: Yes!

PORTER: When, Goddammit, when?

NANCY: Last fall. When he stayed with us after his trip west.

PORTER: *(Walking away)* I don't want to know.

NANCY: O K, you don't have to.

PORTER: *(Wheeling on her)* TELL me!

NANCY: It was a Saturday afternoon...

PORTER: Where were the kids?

NANCY: Out, obviously... So was the dog.

PORTER: I don't give a shit about the dog.

NANCY: That's something new.

PORTER: Go ON, goddammit!

NANCY: You and I had just had another fight, so you'd run off to the Red Sox game, and I thought I'd take a bath and listen to *The Marriage of Figaro*.

PORTER: Where was Chris?

NANCY: I'm trying to *tell* you, Porter… So after our fight, I put on the stereo, and got in the tub, and was listening to that sad aria by the Countess when she feels so alone. *"Dove sono i bei momenti"*… Where are the beautiful moments?

PORTER: I don't give a shit about the beautiful moments.

NANCY: Well I do!

PORTER: Go on, go on.

NANCY: There was a knock on the bathroom door.

PORTER: Chris?

NANCY: He had made me a cup of tea.

PORTER: Goddam British and their fucking tea!

NANCY: If you're going to start stereotyping people again, I won't say another word.

PORTER: No, go on. He brought you tea. What did you say?

NANCY: I said thank you, and please leave it outside the door.

PORTER: And he said?

NANCY: He asked if he could bring it in.

PORTER: WHAT?

NANCY: He said he had always admired my body and wanted to see me naked.

PORTER: And you said?

NANCY: I said O K!

PORTER: Jesus, Nancy!

NANCY: Yes well remember, Porter. Not too many people have made that request recently.

ACT TWO

PORTER: O K. I hear you. Go on.

NANCY: So he came into the bathroom and handed me the tea.

PORTER: And that's all?

NANCY: No. He asked if he could get into the tub with me.

PORTER: That CREEP!

NANCY: The English like to take baths, Porter!

PORTER: Bastard!

NANCY: You've done it, too, Porter. Remember when the Danforths went skinny dipping? You joined right in!

PORTER: All right, all right. Go on!

NANCY: So he took off his clothes and got in. But the tub was too small. American tubs aren't as big as British tubs, Porter. The water was spilling all over the bathroom floor. We could have had a serious leak!

PORTER: Oh really.

NANCY: So we jumped out, and put on our clothes, and toweled up the mess, and then drank tea and listened to the rest of the opera downstairs. And when it was finished we shook hands and he left.

PORTER: That's all?

NANCY: That's all.

PORTER: The guy probably couldn't make it with you anyway.

NANCY: Not true. Not true at all.

PORTER: How you know?

NANCY: You could tell.

PORTER: That bastard.

NANCY: We even discussed it. He said it wouldn't be cricket.

PORTER: "Wouldn't be cricket"? To who? Barbara Birdfeather?

NANCY: To you, ya jerk! And I agreed.

PORTER: This is a bad dream!

NANCY: No, sweetheart, listen. With my Nigerian friend, things happened and it meant nothing. With Chris, nothing happened and it meant everything!

PORTER: Why everything?

NANCY: Because it was all about you... But you know something? I am suddenly terribly, terribly tired. Do you mind if I go to bed?

PORTER: How could you possibly sleep?

NANCY: Because I've finally gotten this off my chest. Coming up?

PORTER: No.

NANCY: Please.

PORTER: I have to think things out.

NANCY: So should I. I should think about...who'd you say it was? Anita?

PORTER: It didn't amount to—

NANCY: I know... But won't it be nice when we don't have to talk about who we've been fooling around with?

PORTER: Nancy...

NANCY: Goodnight, sweetie. I think we're both the better for this. In the long run. Thanks to Chris. *(She goes.)*

(A STUDENT clears the coat-tree.)

ACT TWO

PORTER: *(To audience)* So there I stood, thinking of all the great cuckolds of literature: Agamemnon…King Mark…Lady Chatterley's husband—all those men betrayed by their wives. And I thought those guys were lucky. They at least could kill, or get mad, or something! But me? What could I do? How do you deal with a guy who jumps into the tub with your wife, then jumps out and shakes hands? What do you do? …I didn't get much sleep that weekend, but Monday was Patriot's Day, a state holiday, so I tried to sleep in.

(The sound of a telephone)

PORTER: But guess who telephoned at half past eight. *("Answers" sleepily)* Yes?

(CHRIS *appears in a light somewhere.*)

CHRIS: *(As if on a telephone)* I fear I may have called too early.

PORTER: *(Coldly)* What's on your mind, Chris?

CHRIS: I know how your family scatters on holidays.

PORTER: Yes. You know. You've dwelt among us.

CHRIS: Look, I don't think we should impose our disagreements on the next generation. I wonder if one of your children would like to join me tonight at Symphony Hall. Julia Child will be reading Carl Sandburg's *Portrait of Lincoln*.

PORTER: It's a school night, Chris. I'm going to say no.

CHRIS: How about you then?

PORTER: Julia Child is not quite my meat.

CHRIS: Pity. It would give us a chance to talk.

PORTER: We can talk now.

CHRIS: On the telephone? It would be a far, far better thing to meet face to face.

PORTER: About what?

CHRIS: I hear you recently spoke to the Dean about me.

PORTER: He asked my opinion.

CHRIS: What exactly did you say?

PORTER: It was a private meeting, Chris.

CHRIS: Even in Rhodesia, even a black man has the right to confront his accuser.

PORTER: *(With a sigh)* Where do you want to meet, Chris?

CHRIS: Let me suggest the Minuteman Café, on Boylston Street, at six this evening.

PORTER: I'll be there.

(Music. STUDENTS set up a small table and two bistro chairs. PORTER crosses to the table. CHRIS comes on from the opposite direction.)

PORTER: *(To audience; as he shakes hands with CHRIS)* There was the usual preliminary badinage...

CHRIS & PORTER: *(Simultaneously)* How are Nancy and the children?... How is Barbara?... Fine...just fine... How'd you find this joint?... Good roast beef sandwiches...sit down... Thank you...

(A STUDENT comes up to take their order.)

CHRIS: What would you like to drink?

PORTER: Just a beer, thanks.

CHRIS: I thought you liked scotch.

PORTER: Sometimes I like it too much.

CHRIS: *(To STUDENT)* Jimmy, bring Professor Platt a double malt scotch, please. *(To PORTER)* Ice or no.

PORTER: You win, Chris. I'll be aggressively English. Make it neat.

CHRIS: *(To WAITER)* No ice for the gentleman. Jim... And soda water for me.

ACT TWO

(STUDENT *goes off.*)

PORTER: You're not drinking?

CHRIS: Stomach difficulties. The anxieties that go with my rather tenuous position in the Department. But may we "cut to the chase," as they say in Hollywood.

PORTER: My talk with the Dean.

CHRIS: Did you know that because of my little speech at the faculty meeting, I'm being mentioned to replace him?

PORTER: He mentioned that. Yes. And asked for my opinion. I said I didn't think you were the right man.

CHRIS: Why not?

PORTER: For one thing, you're not qualified, Chris. You don't have your PhD.

CHRIS: I wouldn't need a PhD if I were Dean. The duties are almost entirely administrative.

PORTER: Still.

CHRIS: And I'd just be the Acting Dean. While they look for a more suitable replacement.

PORTER: Still.

CHRIS: I have the total support of the junior faculty. Likewise many of the tenured. The Dean hopes to make it unanimous.

(STUDENT *brings drinks.*)

CHRIS: Thank you, Jimmy.

(STUDENT *goes.*)

CHRIS: But apparently you said you didn't trust me.

PORTER: I said that. Yes.

CHRIS: I hope you're not letting personal feelings stand in the way of a professional judgment.

PORTER: You mean Nancy.

CHRIS: We remembered you and honored you.

PORTER: She told me that.

CHRIS: Have I ever harmed you, Porter? Done you a disservice of any kind?

PORTER: No.

CHRIS: Then why are you harming *me*?

PORTER: I don't want you over me, Chris.

CHRIS: Over?

PORTER: In charge. Making decisions. I think you're an opportunist.

CHRIS: An…?

PORTER: Opportunist. Opportunist.

CHRIS: Would you define that for me, please?

PORTER: *(Drinking)* You use people.

CHRIS: Example, please.

PORTER: O K. Margie Ryan, in Department Headquarters, says you're constantly badgering her for special favors. Office, classrooms, scheduling, all that.

CHRIS: Oh well, Madam Ryan. Our little Irish gatekeeper. I believe she harbors a certain native resentment towards the English.

PORTER: You've used me, Chris.

CHRIS: You?

PORTER: From the beginning. You've used me, and my home, and my family, and my colleagues. Nobody likes to be used. And in the process you've wounded my friend Seymour. *(He downs his drink.)*

CHRIS: Would you like another drink?

PORTER: No thanks.

ACT TWO

CHRIS: Of course you would…Jimmy! *(Signals for another drink for* PORTER*)* Now. As for your friend Seymour, I believe he can take care of himself. As for using you… Has it ever occurred to you, Porter, that you've used me? Bringing me in as some sort of cultural counterweight? Setting me up to do a job you couldn't do yourself?

(The STUDENT *brings* PORTER *another scotch, and goes.)*

CHRIS: And because I've done what you wanted—and done it well, I dare say—you've become jealous and envious. Have you ever looked at things from that perspective?

PORTER: *(Finally)* You have a point.

CHRIS: I believe I do.

PORTER: So that makes us even. Now what?

CHRIS: I'll leave that up to you.

PORTER: You want to bury the hatchet?

CHRIS: Bury the…?

PORTER: Hatchet. Hatchet. It's an old Indian expression. Ask your wife what it means! …No, I'm sorry. That was definitely out of order.

CHRIS: Not at all. She loves tribal lore. In fact, right now she's visiting an aunt on the reservation.

PORTER: Oh really? What reservation?

CHRIS: Greenwich, Connecticut, actually.

*(*CHRIS *and* PORTER *both laugh.)*

PORTER: Oh hell, Chris, let's move on. There's more to life than all this academic bullshit.

*(*PORTER *sweeps his hand across the table, knocks over his drink. He and* CHRIS *both jump to their feet.* STUDENTS *quickly arrive to clean up.)*

PORTER: Sorry. *(Reaches for his wallet)* Let me pay. I did most of the drinking.

CHRIS: Nonsense. This is my party. *(Indicates to STUDENT to put it on his monthly bill)* Thank you, Jimmy.

PORTER: Let's get out of here.

(CHRIS and PORTER leave the bar.)

(Street sounds, evening light)

PORTER: *(Slightly drunk by now)* Hey look, Chris. Look around. Here we are, standing on one of the loveliest streets in one of the loveliest towns in America. It's a gorgeous spring night, and half the youth of America are spilling out onto the front stoops. *(Puts his arm around CHRIS's shoulder)* What say you and I walk down Beacon to the Common, and ogle the babes along the way. There's more to life than climbing the academic ladder to God knows where.

CHRIS: Are you saying that you don't really care whether I'm Dean or not?

PORTER: Not tonight.

CHRIS: May I quote you on that?

PORTER: Quote me to who? *The New York Times*?

CHRIS: I'll walk you to your car.

PORTER: *(Indicating offstage)* It's over there.

CHRIS: *(As PORTER starts off)* Say, do you suppose you could deliver Seymour Blum?

PORTER: Deliver him where? *(He goes off)*

CHRIS: Never mind… *(Calling after him)* Now drive carefully, please. I don't want to be responsible for an accident.

(CHRIS goes off another way, as STUDENTS clear the table and chairs, and NANCY comes out with an ironing board. She irons a dress for a party.)

ACT TWO   77

NANCY: *(Calling toward off)* So what's the deal? Are we supposed to be celebrating the Dean going out, or Chris coming in?

PORTER: *(From off)* Both, I guess.

NANCY: I'm not nuts about these end-of-term parties. All the spouses have to stand around and nod at things we know nothing about. How long do we have to stay?

PORTER: *(From off)* Not long, I promise.

NANCY: I imagine it will be worse this year. Now The Old One-Two has bitten the dust. People will be huddling together in little groups. Tenure, non-tenure, hawks, doves. All eyeing each other furtively.

PORTER: *(From off)* Probably.

NANCY: And I suppose Chris will be working the room. What do we call him now? Dean Simpson? Your Royal Highness? What?

(PORTER *comes on, dressed for the occasion.*)

PORTER: He's just Acting Dean, remember. *(He might zip up her back.)*

NANCY: I'll bet he stays on.

PORTER: *(As she carries out the ironing board)* Maybe so. I hear there have been telephone calls from a Kennedy. But I have to say he's good. At the last faculty meeting, the head of the Artificial Intelligence Lab stood up and asked point-blank, "What good are the Humanities?" So Chris shot back, "What good is a baby?" Everybody applauded.

NANCY: *(Coming back on, taking his arm)* Let's go to the party.

PORTER: *(To audience, as he and* NANCY *cross the stage)* Our Faculty Club is on the top floor of an efficient building, overlooking the Charles River…

(Canned music and party sounds as NANCY *and* PORTER *come into the party)*

NANCY: *(Looking around)* Maybe at last we'll meet Barbara Birdfeather.

PORTER: She's still in the hospital.

NANCY: Hospital?

PORTER: Boston Lying-In. Didn't I tell you? They just had a baby girl. Named Miranda. From *The Tempest*. "O brave new world…"

NANCY: How sweet.

(A STUDENT *in a white jacket passes a tray of white wine.)*

STUDENT: Hi, folks. In ten minutes, you're supposed to gather in the back bar. Dean Simpson has a surprise. *(Goes off.)*

PORTER: Uh oh. Probably more scenes from "Workshop on Will."

NANCY: Spare us.

*(*SEYMOUR *comes on in coat and tie.)*

SEYMOUR: I'd tell you to try the shrimp, but Natalie Katz went through it like Moby Dick through a school of krill.

NANCY: How do you feel about all this, Seymour?

SEYMOUR: Oh, hell, let him rule over us. Administrators are like plumbers anyway. We pay them exorbitantly to do things we don't want to do ourselves.

*(*ANITA *comes up, dressed to the nines.)*

ANITA: I love these parties. I've just met the nicest man from the Department of Metallurgy.

PORTER: What's he doing here?

ACT TWO

ANITA: He wants me to teach him to write. Oh, and I've been talking to Margie Ryan. She said they finally got an answer from Oxford. Chris *did* go there, after all.

PORTER: I didn't know there was a problem.

ANITA: Oh yes. At first they said they had no record of him. But it turns out he took a tutorial on Shakespeare there, before he left to coach rugby at Eton…

SEYMOUR: God's in his heaven, and all's right with the world.

(Another white-jacketed STUDENT *comes on.)*

STUDENT: Everyone to the back bar, please. Dean Simpson is going to play the piano.

SEYMOUR: He's become a true American. Replacing Shakespeare with musical comedy.

*(*ANITA, NANCY, SEYMOUR, *and the* STUDENT *go off.* PORTER *remains.)*

PORTER: *(To audience)* He had written a song. Or at least the lyrics to a song. The tune was "When I Was a Lad," from Gilbert and Sullivan's *Pinafore*. Only he didn't sing about being the ruler of the Queen's nav-ee. He sang about the various people in the department. The rhymes were clever, the satire was friendly, and every verse had a neat little punch line.

(Sounds of hearty laughter)

PORTER: He couldn't mention everybody, of course, but he went through quite a list, and his song was good enough so that there was applause after every verse.

(Sounds of applause)

*(*NANCY *comes out, takes* PORTER's *arm.)*

NANCY: He's saving you till last.

PORTER: Uh oh.

*(*ANITA *joins them.)*

ANITA: *(Whispering)* Wasn't that funny, what he sang about me? ..."Our local Circe... Who shows no mercy..."

PORTER: It was, it was.

(More applause)

(SEYMOUR joins them.)

SEYMOUR: "I hope I may agree more...with Seymour." Not good, but not bad.

ANITA: The spirit of reconciliation is in the air.

SEYMOUR: He's getting close to the end.

(NANCY nudges PORTER, who waits expectantly.)

NANCY: *(To PORTER)* You're next.

(They all turn to watch the next verse.)

PORTER: *(To audience)* But it was a nice verse about the outgoing Dean.

(Then we hear the sound of larger applause, cheering and whistling. "Hear hear," "Right on!" "Bravo!")

NANCY: That's it? That's all?

SEYMOUR: I guess it is.

(CHRIS comes on, dressed to the nines, surrounded by white-jacketed STUDENTS, amid sounds of cheering and applause. ANITA goes up to him and gives him a hug. SEYMOUR shakes his hand. PORTER starts toward CHRIS.)

NANCY: *(Touching his arm)* Don't.

PORTER: Don't what?

NANCY: You're going to do something.

PORTER: What makes you think that?

(CHRIS turns to PORTER.)

CHRIS: Ah, Porter...

ACT TWO

(He smilingly holds out his hand. PORTER *swings a roundhouse punch and sends* CHRIS *reeling into the crowd. Screams and gasps from all)*

(Blackout)

(Music. Lights up on PORTER's *office.* SEYMOUR, *in shirtsleeves, comes on with a stack of cardboard cartons. He begins to pack up the books from the bookcase. After a moment,* ANITA *comes in, now in informal clothes.)*

ANITA: Where's Porter?

SEYMOUR: Meeting with the President.

ANITA: To be fired?

SEYMOUR: Of course.

ANITA: Despite his tenure?

SEYMOUR: The Discipline Committee found him guilty of assault and battery on a fellow faculty member.

ANITA: I'd help you pack him up, but I've got to move myself.

SEYMOUR: Don't tell me they're firing you.

ANITA: Just the reverse. Chris asked me to set up a Writing Center in the old Chemistry Building. There's one glass wall, so people can stroll by and watch us write.

SEYMOUR: Will you be writing about sex?

ANITA: No. I'm over all that. I had a disappointing experience last winter with a caged eagle.

SEYMOUR: Oh?

ANITA: It made me realize that sex is like Dumbo's feather. Once it helped me fly, but now I can teach without it.

SEYMOUR: What will you write about, then?

ANITA: Metallurgy has begun to interest me.

SEYMOUR: That and a letter from Chris will get you tenure.

ANITA: Let's hope. *(She goes.)*

(SEYMOUR packs more books. PORTER comes on. He takes off his jacket and rolls up his sleeves to join in the packing.)

SEYMOUR: So? What did the President say?

PORTER: *(As he packs)* He said Chris is being magnanimous.

SEYMOUR: No lawsuit or anything?

PORTER: All I have to do is make a public apology. And pay for his new set of teeth.

SEYMOUR: Then do it, man!

PORTER: I've already sent the check for the teeth.

SEYMOUR: *(Putting the books back onto the shelves)* Great! You can keep your job.

PORTER: But I don't think I can apologize.

SEYMOUR: Of course you can. Try to understand the man, Porter. If you grew up in a doomed, disintegrating anachronism like Rhodesia, you'd have limited loyalties, too. He's a man without a country. To him, all relationships are strictly political. We know that now, and can live with it now.

PORTER: Can you live with me?

SEYMOUR: Why not? You had good reason to hit him.

PORTER: Because he neglected to mention me in his triumphal song? I wanted to *kill* the son of a bitch! Do I spend the rest of my days wandering through the halls like some Ancient Mariner, trying to explain that to my colleagues—and to myself? *(Starts packing the books again)* I told the President I'm resigning.

SEYMOUR: What? You are resigning tenure at a major institution because you lost your cool?

ACT TWO

PORTER: I'm not right for this place, Seymour. And not right for this profession. You sensed it yourself. I've been spinning my wheels. As Plato says in *The Republic*, most of the evil in the world comes from people being in the wrong slot in life. They mess things up for everyone else.

SEYMOUR: Where in *The Republic* does Plato say that?

PORTER: I'm not sure. See? I'm a lousy scholar…But it's there. And it's true. *(More packing)* Last night, after I made up my mind to leave, Nancy and I had the best time in bed we've had in years.

SEYMOUR: I'm not interested.

PORTER: I am.

SEYMOUR: What'll you do for dough?

PORTER: She's got her degree now. She'll be the breadwinner while I try to write something.

SEYMOUR: I've got your title: *The Rejected Sector*. Colon. *Americans Without Tenure*.

PORTER: Maybe I'll write about all of this.

SEYMOUR: Make it mostly about me. *(Checking his watch)* But hey, look at the time. I should go home and do some packing of my own. We're taking the kids to England for the summer.

PORTER: England?

SEYMOUR: I see England as the last outpost of western civilization.

PORTER: Even after Chris?

SEYMOUR: He's not English. He's a colonial, which makes him a parody of the English. Or rather he's a parody of a colonial, which makes him a parody of a parody. Uh-oh. Two negatives make a positive. He could be the real thing…Maybe we'll go to Las Vegas.

(Starts out) I'll call when we get back. We'll check out *Duck Soup*. *(He goes.)*

(PORTER *packs for a moment, then speaks to audience.*)

PORTER: And then suddenly I became aware that the sound of Margie Ryan's typewriter, down at the end of the hall, had stopped. And I thought of that moment in Faulkner when the hero realizes that a woodpecker has stopped tapping and the Bear is watching him from a thicket nearby.

(CHRIS *appears in the doorway: tan, well-dressed.*)

CHRIS: I beg your pardon.

(PORTER *jumps, turns to see him.*)

CHRIS: Sorry. I thought you heard me.

PORTER: I didn't.

CHRIS: May I come in?

PORTER: Sure.

(CHRIS *comes into the office.*)

PORTER: Back where we started.

CHRIS: Where we…?

PORTER: Started. Me here, you there.

CHRIS: Quite right. Yes. *(Pause)* I want to know why you tried to kill me.

PORTER: I want to know, too…

CHRIS: Somebody said it was not mentioning you in my song.

PORTER: Don't you think I at least deserved a footnote?

CHRIS: A footnote?

PORTER: For getting you started. And helping you along the way.

CHRIS: I hope you did nothing untoward.

ACT TWO

PORTER: Of course not.

CHRIS: I also hope that what little success I've achieved here has had something to do with my own abilities.

PORTER: Oh yes.

CHRIS: And if I've seized the hour, isn't that what one's supposed to do in America? I mean, this is the land of opportunity, isn't it?

PORTER: Oh it is, it is.

CHRIS: Now look: I tried very hard to put you in the song. I labored over several verses—about you, your home, your family. But they didn't work. I couldn't find your...center.

PORTER: O K. Fair enough. I'm just beginning to find it myself.

CHRIS: Perhaps when you do, you'll be less inclined to strike people down when they hold out their hand. The handshake is an ancient gesture of trust. You broke a basic sacrament.

PORTER: You broke something even more basic, Chris.

CHRIS: What? What did I break?

PORTER: You broke the basic law of hospitality.

CHRIS: Oh please.

PORTER: *(Picking up* The Odyssey*)* Back to Homer, buddy. Or even farther—back to the cave. I invited you to warm your hands at my fire. I welcomed you into my family. And when you were all warmed and rested and fed, you went your way without even introducing yourself.

CHRIS: I brought gifts, I was affectionate with your children, I honored your wife.

PORTER: You never came clean, Chris. You came through customs without ever opening your bags.

CHRIS: I have said this before, and I suppose I'll have to keep saying it. If I don't have that delightful American custom of wearing my heart prominently on my sleeve, I hope you'll forgive me. I come from an older and more guarded world. Perhaps when I've lived here longer, I'll be able to strip myself bare and parade my soul in front of every passing stranger.

PORTER: I'm not a stranger, Chris.

CHRIS: We are all strangers, all the time.

PORTER: That I will never agree with! ...But, hell, life's too short to argue. At least we're fellow fathers. Congratulations on the baby.

CHRIS: Thank you.

PORTER: Kids are the heart of the matter. Right, Dad? At least till they reach adolescence.

CHRIS: Mmm.

PORTER: And I apologize for hitting you. I'll put it in writing. That'll clear your deck for next fall.

CHRIS: I won't be here next fall.

PORTER: Won't be here?

CHRIS: Like you, I've just seen the President, and resigned.

PORTER: Why?

CHRIS: Because I'm going up the river.

PORTER: Up the river? *(To audience)* For some reason, I thought of Sing-Sing.

CHRIS: The Charles River, Porter. I've accepted a position at Harvard.

PORTER: Harvard?

CHRIS: A friend put in a word for me. I'll be in charge of career counseling.

ACT TWO

PORTER: At Harvard?

CHRIS: It's a temporary slot, but as you know, so was this... *(Looks at his watch)* Matter of fact, I'm due there now. So goodbye, Porter.

(CHRIS shakes PORTER's hand briskly and goes.)

PORTER: Goddammit, Chris!

(PORTER starts out after CHRIS, runs into NANCY coming in, shaking out an umbrella)

NANCY: Hey! Watch it.

PORTER: Which way did he go?

NANCY: Who?

PORTER: Chris.

NANCY: Don't know, and don't care.

PORTER: *(Rushing out)* I feel like hitting him again.

NANCY: Don't bother.

PORTER: *(Looking around)* He's gone.

NANCY: See? You'd be swinging at nothing but thin air.

PORTER: You're right.

NANCY: So. Did you follow through with the President?

PORTER: I did. I quit.

NANCY: Good! Now you can finish your novel.

PORTER: I'm thinking of writing about this.

NANCY: Really? Well let's go. The kids are waiting in the car. They'll help with the books if we buy them lunch. I said O K, as long as nobody orders junk food.

PORTER: You mean they'll eat with us? In public?

NANCY: If we don't embarrass them—by talking.

PORTER: It's a deal.

(NANCY *and* PORTER *start out. Then* PORTER *stops.*)

NANCY: What's the matter?

PORTER: *(Looking back at his office)* Maybe not a novel but a play...

NANCY: A play? Will audiences care about this stuff?

PORTER: *(Glancing toward the audience)* They might... If I can figure out an ending.

NANCY: *(Taking his arm)* Short and sweet is my motto. *(A quick kiss)* Now move it. Before the kids change their minds.

(NANCY *puts up her umbrella as they go off under it together.*)

(*Music: spirited and optimistic*)

END OF PLAY

www.ingramcontent.com/pod-product-compliance
Lightning Source LLC
Chambersburg PA
CBHW071728040426
42446CB00011B/2266